BREAKING BARRIERS

VOLUME TWO

EXERCISING THE BARRIER BREAKER'S ANOINTING

CROSSING THE LINE OF LIFE'S LIMITATIONS

MATTHEW ASHIMOLOWO

© 2001 Matthew Ashimolowo

Published by Mattyson Media an imprint of MAMM
Matthew Ashimolowo Media Ministries
57 Waterden Road
Hackney Wick
London
E15 2EE
ISBN 1 874 646 481

Bible quotes are from the King James Bible
unless otherwise stated as the following:

Appreciation is expressed to the following publishers for sections of
translations reprinted:

A Rendering of the Book of Psalms (John De Witt)
The Holy Bible: A Translation from the Latin Vulgate in the Light of
Hebrew and Greek Originals (Monsignor Ronald Knox)
A Translation of the Old Testament Scriptures (Helen Spurrell)
The Septuagint (Charles Thomson)
The New American Bible
The Bible: An American Translation (J M Powis Smith)
The Holy Bible From Ancient Easten Manuscripts (George M Lansa)
The Jerusalem Bible
The Revised Standard Version of the Bible
The Bible in Basic English
The Amplified Bible
P.8 quoted from "101 Great Laws of Success" Matthew Ashimolowo
© 1999 Matthew Ashimolowo Media Ministries

CONTENTS

INTRODUCTION

Following my book on the first subject "Breaking Barriers", it is necessary for us to see some other barriers the enemy tries to raise, and the power available to bring them down.

But you must understand that
Satan's chief desire is to keep you where you are,
that is why he erects barriers, that is why he raises up fences.

The biggest problem the enemy has is that he knows that with God on your side, there is nothing you cannot achieve.

And the LORD said, Behold, the people is one, and they have all one language; and this they begin to do: and now nothing will be restrained from them, which they have imagined to do.
Genesis 11:6 (KJV)

His chief desire is to keep you from maximising whom God called you to be; he builds as many walls that can hold you. Satan never expected you to come this far, he thought you should have failed a long time ago, but through Christ you have been brought this far.

The story is told often times of the proverbial louse that was put in a jar with a lid on the top, who jumped as hard as it could to get out of the jar. But every time it did, it hit the lid and went back to the bottom. After several attempts the louse must have been conditioned, because when the lid was removed, the louse's jump was always to the level where the lid used to be. Though the lid was now removed, the lid was registered on his mind.

Satan's chief tool often times is containment; but he contains people by giving them a sense of contentment with their present level.

Then contentment, which produces containment, results in a comfort zone.

Progress stops when you are contained.

You never reach another level; you never achieve beyond where you used to be. Visions perish in the zone of comfort; people give up and believe they have achieved all they can, and they attribute their present comfort zone to the fact that, that was where God was bringing them to. So their own achievements, and the containment of the enemy holds them and limits the level they could ever reach.

The enemy of our faith knows fully well that if you can be precluded from seeing your potential and your harvest, you would be satisfied with where you are now.

Containment will make a person with a birthright live like a beggar. It will make a man who is so blessed to continue to live in bondage.

Barriers of the mind are the only things one can blame.

For example the children of Israel who wanted to go back and eat leeks and garlic, when their ordination was for milk and honey.

My dear friend, you are too good for the limitations that the enemy tries to put on you. It is time to engage the weapons of our warfare that are mighty through God to the pulling down of barriers and strongholds, so you can enter and possess the favour you were ordained to enjoy.

Your destiny is so strong it scares the devil, your destiny is so awesome it send quivers to the corners of hell, your destiny is so great it gives the devil diarrhoea. They catch a headache in hell, every time you wake up. But what God is set to do in your life, the devil cannot stop it, he cannot stand it, yet there is nothing he can do about it.

CHAPTER ONE

Pastor Bakka
078 532 44990

BREAKING SATANIC BARRIERS

The chief reason why Satan builds barriers to try to stop you is because he knows you are capable of achieving God's purpose and programme for your life.

God achieves all His programmes, and He created us in His own image to be achievers, champions and overcomers in this life. Before our battles began He declared us winners.

Nay, in all these things we are more than conquerors
through him that loved us.
Romans 8:37 (KJV)

But if you must break the barriers, you must first understand them.

The enemy works so hard to try to stop you. In Isaiah 45:1-3, we see the intentions of the enemy against King Cyrus. Bible scholars say that the prophecy concerning the barriers he was to face and the victory he was to enjoy preceded his birth.

Thus saith the LORD to his anointed, to Cyrus, whose
right hand I have holden, to subdue nations before him;
and I will loose the loins of kings, to open before him the
two leaved gates; and the gates shall not be shut;
I will go before thee, and make the crooked places
straight: I will break in pieces the gates of brass, and cut
in sunder the bars of iron:
And I will give thee the treasures of darkness, and hidden
riches of secret places, that thou mayest know that I, the
LORD, which call thee by thy name, am the God of Israel.
Isaiah 45:1-3 (KJV)

So the enormity of the battle also determines the greatness of God's arsenal released, so that you can enjoy total victory.

TYPES OF BARRIERS

WALLS

Walls were used in Bible times for protection of cities and properties. But they are often used symbolically in Scripture as tools of satanic oppression. Certainly whatever is held within a wall is meant to be limited, so that no one can come in and no one can go out.

Now Jericho was straitly shut up because of the children of Israel: none went out, and none came in. And the LORD said unto Joshua, See, I have given into thine hand Jericho, and the king thereof, and the mighty men of valour.
Joshua 6:1-2 (KJV)

Walls are raised by the enemy to limit and bring restrictions upon your life.

Anything which tries to limit your reach; socially, emotionally, spiritually, and educationally is an invisible wall, it is a barrier. But the anointing must come against it and the wall must fall flat.

Walls try to define you, because if you can be confined, then you can be defined.

A young man was sent to pick me at Dulles Airport in Washington, to take me to the hotel I was to stay, as I ministered for a church in College Park, Maryland. This was approximately one hour's drive. When we reached our destination, the young man was surprised that I was not impressed with how long it took to drive to the hotel.

He told me the story of how when he first came from one of the Polynesian Islands to the United States. He recalled that after one hour's drive when they got to the home of his hosts, he thought they had reached the end of the United States of America, because the island from where he comes only takes thirty minutes from boundary to boundary.

Walls try to define and draw the line of your future, and the enemy knows that if he can limit your future, he would also limit the future of the generations to come through you. That is why satanic walls must come down.

Walls hold people in slavery; mental walls will make you a mental slave, unable to explore and fulfil your vision.

It is not enough that you are born-again, it is Satan's desire to make you a lame duck. But the barrier must come down, for the anointing will speak against it.

The spirit that possessed Pharaoh, but which let the Children of Israel go must have been the same spirit that tried to confine them within the boundaries of the wilderness. The enemy is working so hard to hold you within certain limits, but it is time to be unlimited.

You were called to enjoy the Eden; before you the walls must come down.

You were called to benefit from all that is in Canaan; Jericho walls must not stop you. You cannot keep living in Egypt and keep barely getting along; you must aspire and go beyond the limit. Take all that is for you, the barriers must not stop you.

You cannot even give the walls as an excuse for lack of achieving. You have the tools with which to bring them down, which we shall consider in the subsequent chapters.

When people live within the walls, they just feel hopeless, though they can see a life beyond where they are. To be limited by the walls is to be barely getting along; living in debt, eating leeks and garlic, while the food you were ordained to eat is within reach, but the walls are stopping you.

Walls are ugly situations, tragedies and experiences that make monsters out of beautiful people.

Walls make prisoners out of those who are supposed to inherit a promise that is unfading.

To an inheritance incorruptible, and undefiled, and that fadeth not away, reserved in heaven for you,
1 Peter 1:4 (KJV)

Satan's chief desire is to keep you in the land of limitation, where nothing ever happens.

He likes you to live in a land called "broke", he thinks it is your second name.

All Satan wants is to turn your paradise of plenty to a nightmare.

Those who stay away too long from their vision become a prey to the enemy.

When you stay away too long from what belongs to you, your property becomes the dwelling place of squatters.

If you do not occupy what belongs to you, you cannot stop demonic activity; you cannot stop Satan and his cohorts from encroaching.

If you allow him to hold you in a comfort zone, he will make the wrong people to build on your land.

While Israel languished in the wilderness, their land of fruitfulness was occupied by parasites called the Perrizites, the Jebusites, the Amorites and the Canaanites. There is no greater curse than for you to have a harvest somewhere, but you go to bed with an empty stomach, elsewhere.

Satanic walls makes others replace you in the land where you should have excelled. Somebody is busy eating the milk and honey that belongs to you, while you are in slavery in another land for four hundred and thirty years.

Babylonian walls were built to hold you in slavery, but they must fall.

Babylon is suddenly fallen and destroyed: howl for her; take balm for her pain, if so be she may be healed.
Jeremiah 51:8 (KJV)

Satan's broken walls were supposed to hold you down, and though they were already fallen, they give the impression they are still there, but you will have total victory.

Who art thou, O great mountain? before Zerubbabel thou shalt become a plain: and he shall bring forth the headstone thereof with shoutings, crying, Grace, grace unto it.
Zecheriah 4:7 (KJV)

The walls of Jericho may be huge, it may have stopped generations from coming in. Your property is within the city, go in and possess your possessions.

> *By faith the walls of Jericho fell down, after they were*
> *compassed about seven days.*
> *Hebrews 11:30 (KJV)*

All you need is to express faith and know that
what was meant to stop you, will end up being for
your prosperity.

> *Peace be within thy walls, and prosperity within thy*
> *palaces.*
> *Psalms 122:7 (KJV)*

What was meant to stop you, will become your
wall of salvation.

> *In that day shall this song be sung in the land of Judah;*
> *We have a strong city; salvation will God appoint for walls*
> *and bulwarks.*
> *Isaiah 26:1 (KJV)*

Walls, walls, walls.

It is in the hand of the man whose being
"barriered", to seek his deliverance. Pharaoh
does not want you to go, but righteous indignation,
coupled with fervent prayer means that you must
break out of that jail.

Break out of that spiritual and
mental jail, you were not meant to

be inside when Jesus declared your freedom.

If the Son therefore shall make you free, ye shall be free indeed.
John 8:36 (KJV)

My friend, it is a new day. It is time for you to declare your freedom from comfort zone limitation and Satan's straight jacket. You are too good for Satan's mess, it is time to move from promise to possession.

If God says He gives you power to get wealth, you will not settle for less.

But thou shalt remember the LORD thy God: for it is he that giveth thee power to get wealth.....
Deuteronomy 8:18 (KJV)

Develop a holy dissatisfaction for anything less. There is more to possess than you have ever had.

Make this declaration now.
Satan's wall shall fall, and his lies shall be exposed. Healing belongs to me. Joy belongs to me. Gladness follows me. The enemy's wall must fall. I refuse to be stopped, I will not be

stopped by the walls; I will not be stopped by lack, I will not be stopped by debt, I will not be stopped by need, and I will not be stopped by comfort zones.

GATES

Whoever builds a gate is the one who is the most scared.

Gates were used in Bible times for control and limiting what comes in or goes out of a city. It provided security for the people within, but it is also a symbol of a barrier the enemy can put on the life of the believer.

The instances where gates are mentioned negatively in the Bible could also have a symbolic meaning as the barriers Christians face. We read in Genesis 19:1 of the *'gates of Sodom'*. That symbolically represents everything that is immoral and ungodly that can create a barrier to the blessing of God in your life.

And there came two angels to Sodom at even; and Lot sat in the gate of Sodom:....
Genesis 19:1 (KJV)

Until they are dealt with, they limit the favour that flows to you. Righteousness is a force that provokes the blessing of the Lord.

Genesis 24:60 then talks of the *'gates of those who hate you and your children'*. The gates of hatred can also mean that barriers will be raised against your life by those whose who do not want to see your progress, but as the Word of God predicts, the believer has victory before the barriers were raised.

> .....*and let thy seed possess the gate of those which hate them.*
> *Genesis 24:60 (KJV)*

Jesus talked of the *'gates of hell'* in Matthew 16:18. Twice the Scriptures refer to the *'gates of brass and the bars of iron'*.

> *And I say also unto thee, That thou art Peter, and upon this rock I will build my church; and the gates of hell shall not prevail against it.*
> *Matthew 16:18 (KJV)*

> *I will go before thee, and make the crooked places straight: I will break in pieces the gates of brass, and cut in sunder the bars of iron:*
> *Isaiah 45:2 (KJV)*

> *Oh that men would praise the LORD for his goodness, and for his wonderful works to the children of men!*
> *For he hath broken the gates of brass, and cut the bars of iron in sunder.*
> *Psalms 107:15-16 (KJV)*

God in these two passages declares His intention. He says *"I will break in pieces the gates of brass, and cut in sunder the bars of iron"*. These things may rise against the believer. He need not be afraid because God has already made His intention known. Everything put together against you will not work. Gates may be barriers but they cannot hold you forever. Every brass of impudence, every brass or effrontery, every brass of resistance must crumble in the Name of the Lord.

The interesting thing about the word gate in the Hebrew *shaar* is that not only could it be interpreted as *gate*, it can also be interpreted as *gatekeepers*.

Gatekeepers who want to stop you from making progress; gatekeepers who want to declare to your coming blessings that you do not need them and that they should be taken elsewhere, must receive their sacking. All that God promised you will come within your reach.

Gates were meant to draw lines with the hope that you will not dare to cross. Gates were meant to be unusual challenges, hoping that you will be discouraged, distracted,

divided, denied, demoted and disturbed, and his final intention is to destroy.

This book does not align with Satan, there is no agreement at all with him. Rather God's Word stands, so that the weapon of the enemy would not prevail.

No weapon that is formed against thee shall prosper; and every tongue that shall rise against thee in judgment thou shalt condemn. This is the heritage of the servants of the LORD, and their righteousness is of me, saith the LORD.
Isaiah 54:17 (KJV)

BARS OF IRON

Though they are not mentioned several times, they are very specific to holding back people who were not meant to enter certain towns or cities. They are also symbolic of things the enemy will do to try to hold a believer from entering and maximising the purpose of God for his life.

And it was told Saul that David was come to Keilah. And Saul said, God hath delivered him into mine hand; for he is shut in, by entering into a town that hath gates and bars.
1 Samuel 23:7 (KJV)

In the passage mentioned, attempts were made to stop David from escaping from a city that he had entered, where his enemies were waiting for him.

Some things make you feel as if you have been cornered and there is no way out, but the God who breaks the iron bars still reigns in the affairs of His people, and when He turns the bar of hindrance around, it becomes your testimony.

Oh that men would praise the LORD for his goodness, and for his wonderful works to the children of men!
For he hath broken the gates of brass, and cut the bars of iron in sunder.
Psalms 107:15-16 (KJV)

MOUNTAINS

The City of Jerusalem sat upon many mountains. That geographical location became symbolic in influencing many of the scriptural connotations. One of which is the picture of the battles and challenges that people face.

A mountain is meant to be a picture of a very major barrier which in the natural was thought to be impossible to move. Yet God gives prophetic words like Isaiah 40:4.

*Every valley shall be exalted, and every mountain and hill
shall be made low: and the crooked shall be made straight,
and the rough places plain:*
Isaiah 40:4 (KJV)

God says He will make them low, and if He said
it, it will happen. It was characteristic of people
in Palestine in Bible times to pull down a
mountain if a king was travelling on that path.
Well today we have been ordained kings and
priests to our God, and anything on our way
would have to move. Challenges of life are often
described as mountains, but God tells us they can
move.

We know they can move because firstly, they have
no right to stop us.

*Who art thou, O great mountain? before Zerubbabel thou
shalt become a plain: and he shall bring forth the
headstone thereof with shoutings, crying, Grace, grace
unto it.*
Zechariah 4:7 (KJV)

We must announce our intention to
the mountain itself. "Who are you
O Mountain?". Then we must
declare where the mountain must go.

As far as the Word of God goes, there is only one place for the mountain to go where it can be totally covered and obscured. Throwing it into the sea to a place where it can be found no more.

Therefore will not we fear, though the earth be removed, and though the mountains be carried into the midst of the sea;
Psalms 46:2 (KJV)

For verily I say unto you, That whosoever shall say unto this mountain, Be thou removed, and be thou cast into the sea; and shall not doubt in his heart, but shall believe that those things which he saith shall come to pass; he shall have whatsoever he saith.
Mark 11:23 (KJV)

There are mountains that seem unmoveable; what we need is to come to the presence of the Lord and they shall melt like wax before Him.

The hills melted like wax at the presence of the LORD, at the presence of the Lord of the whole earth.
Psalms 97:5 (KJV)

If they do not melt, they had better get ready to begin to skip like rams.

The mountains skipped like rams, and the little hills like lambs.
Psalms 114:4 (KJV)

God said He would thresh your mountains and make them small. He is able. It does not matter what the problem is, do not call it special. If any problem becomes special, you specialised it! It is time for the battle of life to be taken over easily by the Lord.

When thou didst terrible things which we looked not for, thou camest down, the mountains flowed down at thy presence.
Isaiah 64:3 (KJV)

All you need to do is learn by reason of the anointing to speak to the mountain that you are facing.

Tell it to go the way it came. If it came in written form, it must go back in that form. It must be humbled by the Word.

STORMS

We are told by oceaneologists that storms are caused when the winds collide upon the sea and the tectonic plates of the earth begin to move, thus moving the billions of gallons of water that rest upon them. And when the wind is over and the movement of the tectonic plates is over, the waters go back to be as calm as they used to be.

If you have been caught in a natural storm, you first wonder when it would stop and when will things go back to normal.

Storms are used several times in Scripture to give a picture; every account of natural storms in the Bible gives a picture of something terrifying, which gets even adults afraid for their lives. From the apostles to Jonah, and from Paul, we can see those terrifying moments of life when even the strong is tempted to doubt.

The first thing the believer needs to settle in his mind is that, yes storms are a barrier. But even so, the presence of storms does not in any way indicate that God is absent. If you do not face a challenge, you would not know that God can make you overcome it. If you do not have a need, you will have no testimony as to how God meets such a need. If you have no questions, you would not find the answers.

The presence of storms does not mean that you were not sent. You may be right in the middle of the storm, because the enemy's intention is to stop you from fulfilling your assignment.

Storms are sent to interrupt your journey and to abort your destiny and assignment.

Satan would send the windy storms of life.

> *I would hasten my escape from the windy storm and*
> *tempest.*
> *Psalms 55:8 (KJV)*

He would send the destructive storms of life.

> *Behold, the Lord hath a mighty and strong one, which as a*
> *tempest of hail and a destroying storm, as a flood of*
> *mighty waters overflowing, shall cast down to the earth*
> *with the hand.*
> *Isaiah 28:2 (KJV)*

Satan would send the great storms of life.

> *And there arose a great storm of wind, and the waves beat*
> *into the ship, so that it was now full.*
> *Mark 4:37 (KJV)*

You may be confronted with the storms of jeopardy.

> *But as they sailed he fell asleep: and there came down a storm of wind on the lake; and they were filled with water, and were in jeopardy.*
> *Luke 8:23 (KJV)*

But no matter what you go through, even if your storm has no name. Remember to keep calm and keep the remembrance that God is always good.

> *He maketh the storm a calm, so that the waves thereof are still.*
> *Psalms 107:29 (KJV)*

One of the best places to know God and to remember that He is your Stronghold in the day of trouble, and that no storm is powerful enough to destroy you, is when you go through it.

> *The LORD is slow to anger, and great in power, and will not at all acquit the wicked: the LORD hath his way in the whirlwind and in the storm, and the clouds are the dust of his feet.*
> *Nahum 1:3 (KJV)*

When the storms of life are raging, and you do not know where to turn. The barrier breaker anointing will cause God to stand by you and be your refuge from the storm.

*For thou hast been a strength to the poor, a strength to
the needy in his distress, a refuge from the storm, a
shadow from the heat, when the blast of the terrible ones is
as a storm against the wall.*
Isaiah 25:4 (KJV)

The twelve disciples came face to face with what
seemed would eat them up, and all Jesus did was
to speak to the storm itself. You may go through
the eye of the storm and sometimes Jesus may not
be in the boat, like the occasion when He was
absent.

And even while you are dealing with the storm
you may face a greater battle; like when they saw
Him on the waters and took Him for a ghost. As
they screamed "Phantasma, Phantasma", little did
they realise that the One who would save them is
the One they called a ghost.

The One who would save them, they thought was a greater storm.

For those fishermen on that day in a boat on a
stormy sea; knew that at worst they would swim
to shore - they were fishermen by experience, but
they had never been confronted with a ghost who
walked the waters.

The Barrier Breakers anointing is strong and big enough to deal with even the things that do not have a name as yet.

THE SPIRIT OF FAILURE

There are other barriers we may not expand in this book as we have already covered a few of them, but the spirit of failure is certainly a major barrier that holds our generation, and we will do a disservice if we do not consider it.

This is probably the most confused generation. Technologically advanced; great successes, giant leaps for mankind, and yet the one that has produced, is a generation that gives up so soon if anything does not deliver instantly.

If anything has held many in the greatest bondage, if any barrier has become the strait jacket in which many have not been able to break away, it would be the spirit of failure.

How may I describe this spirit? It is not hard to tell when a person is under its control.

Where the spirit of failure abounds there will be activity without focus, indifference in the face of opportunity, and the inability to control a destructive appetite; drug addiction and all other addictions. A refusal to move away from a bad childhood experience that has paralysed an area of life. The fear of man which brings a snare; a persistent hiding behind the argument of lacking enough education, the inability to be persistent until the battle is won.

Do you want to know what constitutes the spirit of failure? It is emotion without control, it is demanding from life what you have not paid for.

The spirit of failure is mirrored by poor choices of jobs, career, relationships, and poor choices of marriage partners.

Where there is a spirit of failure, there will be a double-minded life, a refusal to take risks.

A pathological fear that paralyses and stops one from making any move. Sticking to things that do not work, a persistent putting of oneself down, being the devil's best advocate against your own life.

Failure is only a tool that is good if it helps you to overcome bad habits. Failure is only a good tool, if it helps you learn how to do better.

Failure is only good if you learn that it is an event - not a person, an attitude or an outcome. Failure is only good if it teaches you and adds to your experience.

But when it is a spirit, the barrier it creates must immediately be broken for they are very severe. One of the barriers the spirit of failure creates is depression.

And all the congregation lifted up their voice, and cried;
and the people wept that night.
Numbers 14:1 (KJV)

A constant complaining about life without any sense of thanks, thankfulness or satisfaction.

And all the children of Israel murmured against Moses and
against Aaron: and the whole congregation said unto them,
Would God that we had died in the land of Egypt! or
would God we had died in this
wilderness!
Numbers 14:2 (KJV)

Suicide tendencies and a persistent attitude of a feeling of persecution.

And all the children of Israel murmured against Moses and against Aaron: and the whole congregation said unto them, Would God that we had died in the land of Egypt! or would God we had died in this wilderness! And wherefore hath the LORD brought us unto this land, to fall by the sword, that our wives and our children should be a prey? were it not better for us to return into Egypt?
Numbers 14:2-3 (KJV)

The spirit of failure will make you turn against God and put on fear and cowardice.

And wherefore hath the LORD brought us unto this land, to fall by the sword, that our wives and our children should be a prey? were it not better for us to return into Egypt?
Numbers 14: 3 (KJV)

The spirit of failure will make a man turn in rebellion and violence against God's authority, and everything around him.

And wherefore hath the LORD brought us unto this land, to fall by the sword, that our wives and our children should be a prey? were it not better for us to return into

> *Egypt? And they said one to another, Let us make a*
> *captain, and let us return into Egypt. But all the*
> *congregation bade stone them with stones.....*
> *Numbers 14:3, 4, 10 (KJV)*

Its final outcome is to leave you as a poor dejected soul, without any sense of being a man called to dominion. It must be clear and sounding in your spirit, that because you are ordained for dominion, anything that tries to hold you must go.

Barriers must be broken, because you are too good for their holding.

You must be released to go and fulfil the destiny which you carry inside you.

How may a man break free from the spirit of failure? It will start by refusing to measure yourself through other people's eyes. That is what the children of Israel did when they saw the size of the people of Jericho. Failing to realise its not who you are, its whose you are.

Create a mental image of Jesus the deliverer, see Him breaking the barriers and removing the shackles from your life.

See yourself free; do not work at becoming a clone of someone else.

You are beautiful for your situation and distinguished for your calling. You are not permitted to imitate.

You were chosen to stand out. Be bold, be strong, for the Lord your God is with you. Take authority over the spirit of failure and declare. My Father is not a failure, Jesus is not a failure, the Holy Ghost is not a failure, and I am surrounded by a company of believers who have a testimony of victory. I am a stranger to failure, and I am too good for its gripping.

THE BARRIERS INTENTION

Why would Satan spend so much time in fighting a believer? Why do you face so much hassles in life? Why are some of us particular targets of the host of hell? It is clear and obvious that nobody attacks tramps. To direct armoured cars at a molehill is to misuse your ammunition. Satan creates barriers according to the level of his understanding of your future ability. The possibilities are there, and he has had a peep into your destiny and he sees it is so bright, it is blinding to him, so he wants to stop you from reaching where you are going.

From Genesis to Calvary, the reason he tried to crush the Seed of the woman is purely because in Him lies the salvation of mankind. Man would live forever because of the woman's Seed. He fought her Seed from Genesis, he tried to extirpate Him in Exodus, he tried to ruin Him in Numbers, and he did not succeed in Deuteronomy. In Judges he brought anarchy, and on and on until Calvary.

He thought he had Him at Calvary when the Son of God died.

But little did he know that His death was part of the programme for the breaking of the final barriers.

Satan's intention is to cause you setbacks to hinder your progress in life and cause you a loss of focus.

Satan's intention is to create barriers and stop you from receiving your healing.

The harvest is past, the summer is ended, and we are not saved. For the hurt of the daughter of my people am I hurt; I am black; astonishment hath taken hold on me. Is there no balm in Gilead; is there no physician there? why then is not the health of the daughter of my people recovered?
Jeremiah 8:20-22 (KJV)

Satan's intention and his barriers are intended to cause you financial setbacks.

Ye have sown much, and bring in little; ye eat, but ye have not enough; ye drink, but ye are not filled with drink; ye clothe you, but there is none warm; and he that earneth wages earneth wages to put it into a bag with holes. Thus saith the LORD of hosts; Consider your ways.
Go up to the mountain, and bring wood, and build the house; and I will take pleasure in it, and I will be glorified, saith the LORD. Ye looked for much, and, lo, it

came to little; and when ye brought it home, I did blow upon it. Why? saith the LORD of hosts. Because of mine house that is waste, and ye run every man unto his own house. Therefore the heaven over you is stayed from dew, and the earth is stayed from her fruit.
Haggai 1:6-10 (KJV)

Satan's intention in sending barriers your way and drawing lines he expects you not to cross, is so that he can create marital problems, rocky marriages, growth-less homes, homes without joy or blessing. He loves it where there is no victory, no testimony and life is in a state of a stand still.

The devil does not have the final say; it is the counsel of the Lord that shall stand.

CHAPTER 2

THE BARRIER BREAKER'S ARSENAL

Paul declared that the battle the believer confronts is not natural, but spiritual.

(For the weapons of our warfare are not carnal, but mighty through God to the pulling down of strong holds;) Casting down imaginations, and every high thing that exalteth itself against the knowledge of God, and bringing into captivity every thought to the obedience of Christ;
2 Corinthians 10:4-5 (KJV)

He had an insight into the fact that the barriers we are facing require a weapon beyond this world for effective victory.

The arsenal available to us is able to pull down every stronghold and anything that rises against the believer. But we must know it, so we can use it.

TYPES OF WEAPONS

Firstly, let us consider the weapon of prayer.

PRAYER

We live at a time of increasing challenges; barriers facing families and individuals. It is also a time of great privilege, the privilege of being able to effectively confront modern problems with supernatural answers. This challenging time gives us the opportunity to discover the importance of prayer.

Prayer is the believer's opportunity to verbalise the needs he has before God; it is the breath of our spirit, the oxygen of the spirit man. Without it we would be dead. Prayer is the food the spirit eats. It is that which gives stamina to the inner man.

But ye, beloved, building up yourselves on your most holy faith, praying in the Holy Ghost,
Jude 1:20 (KJV)

The barriers before you are intended to stop you from God's vision and purposes.

But prayer becomes the conveyor belt that both takes you to your supply and brings God's showers from above. Prayer is like Jacob's ladder, connecting you with heaven - connecting heaven with you.

No prayer - no barrier breaking.
Little prayer - little barrier breaking.

Lots of prayer - lots of breaking of the barriers. Prayer creates intimacy with God. It is the place where we learn the language of heaven and address God by our new status "Abba Father".

Prayer is a mine full of eternal riches of wealth untold and unmined. Prayer

is where we get the result that changes our story.

We must not surrender the fight to pray.
The barriers remain until the believer grabs the battle-axe of prayer and sets its weight to the root of the barrier.

Prayer is your tool for obtaining dominion in this world.

Potentially and positionally we have been given the right to exercise dominion. We have already been told also that as Christ is, so are we in this world.

Herein is our love made perfect, that we may have boldness in the day of judgment: because as he is, so are we in this world.
1 John 4:17 (KJV)

But the manifestation of that truth is only by boldly speaking forth what we want to see God do. Prayer touches heaven, then heaven touches the earth.

Prayer is the one thing that can touch the One whose hand can hold

the whole world, so that He can touch the part of the world where we need a change.

Prayer is the believer's staff to walk in the darkness of this world.

Darkness may be a barrier with some people, but with prayer it cannot stop you. It is the believer's battle-axe so that as we come against the enemy, he bows because of this awesome anointing.

It is the believer's spear; the Old Testament is full of warriors who went to battle with sword and spear.

While the sword represents the Word of God, the spear pierces the heart of the problem; it is thrown ahead of the warrior to the place he cannot go. In the same vein, prayer can go to places and parts we may not be able to reach naturally, and burst the gathering storm.

Prayer is the weapon the Lord has given the church to send into the eye of the storm, and quell the storm while it is still gathering.

Prayer is our future. No prayer, no future. Prayer makes your place in dominion possible and effective.

But ye are a chosen generation, a royal priesthood, an holy nation, a peculiar people; that ye should shew forth the praises of him who hath called you out of darkness into his marvellous light:
1 Peter 2:9 (KJV)

It is important to the Christian life; it is that tear that falls without being unnoticed. It is your upward glance to Heaven to get the Father's attention. It is the cry of a child to a Father. It is one thing barriers know and respect. Satan may not stop you from reading the Bible or doing several things, but he knows and he fights the spirit of prayer.

Prayer is our last word before we pass over; it was the last thing Jesus said before He crossed into eternity.

And when Jesus had cried with a loud voice, he said, Father, into thy hands I commend my spirit: and having said thus, he gave up the ghost.
Luke 23:46 (KJV)

Three and half years of drought in the days of Elijah, and yet the man of God throws his arms towards heaven again.

Prayer was what broke the brassy skies and caused rain to fall upon the earth, changing a dry arid desert land; changing a land where the winds blew and the sky became covered with dust, to the one so lush and green, as nature responded to the cry of one man.

THE NAME OF JESUS

We read in Philippians 2:9-10, that Jesus at His resurrection was given a Name that is above all names.

Wherefore God also hath highly exalted him, and given him a name which is above every name: That at the name of Jesus every knee should bow, of things in heaven, and things in earth, and things under the earth;
Philippians 2:9-10 (KJV)

We also read of His Name at birth. It therefore means that Jesus got His Name by the three ways people get great names.

1. They are either born to a great name - as He is born the Son of God.
2. Jesus also inherited a great Name.
3. And the Name was conferred upon Him upon His resurrection.

The Name was given to Jesus for the church to benefit from. Jesus taught us that whatever we ask using His Name, if we believe, we would receive. This in effect means we are given the power of attorney to act on earth fully as Jesus would have acted using His Name. We have the right to use that Name against our enemies; in the presentation of our petition in our times of worship and praise, and as we come against the barriers that the enemy dispatches against us.

The Name of Jesus is one awesome weapon that destabilises Satan's kingdom.

And having spoiled principalities and powers, he made a shew of them openly, triumphing over them in it.
Colossians 2:15 (KJV)

It is the will of the Father that we should humble the devil and all the barriers he puts on our way. All that Jesus was, is encapsulated in that Name.

So when you call upon His Name, you have fully invoked every power available through Jesus Christ. The Name is inseparably connected to our salvation. It is by that Name that we are able to approach God to ask. It is the Name recognised in the Bank of Heaven to make the needs of men met.

> *Neither is there salvation in any other: for there is none other name under heaven given among men, whereby we must be saved.*
> *Acts 4:12 (KJV)*

Public and private identification in water baptism is to be in that Name.

Jesus Himself taught that whatever we desire from the Father, must be presented by the only Name recognised in Heaven.

> *And whatsoever ye shall ask in my name, that will I do, that the Father may be glorified in the Son.*
> *If ye shall ask any thing in my name, I will do it.*
> *John 14:13-14 (KJV)*

There is no barrier strong enough to withstand the awesome power contained in the Name, because all that Jesus is, is represented in that Name. That is why demonic forces are not strong in their ganging up to stop its power and efficacy.

Over one hundred and thirty times the Bible would say "In His Name", or "In Christ", to make us understand our legal standing.

Fasting is great for channelling our mind and spirit to focus on God in prayer, but what carries power is the Name of Jesus. For it is the Name that we have been given with the backing of Heaven to perform wonders on earth.

Once you know the power in the Name, then you must confront the mountain, the Name of Jesus is enough.

Sickness, circumstance, Satan or situations beyond your ability to explain, must bow because of what it knows, that there is power in the Name.

There is no reason to be controlled by weakness, or to see barrenness as a barrier you cannot overcome.

There is no reason to live a powerless Christian life. The Name of Jesus becomes your power to confront the impossible. The use of the Name does not require any faith on your part. He gave it to you, it is yours, and as you confront situations, there has to be a change.

In Genesis 17:1-4 God reveals Himself as El-Shaddai to Abraham. In English, the most appropriate interpretation of this Name is "Almighty God". Take note that Abraham at this time was ninety-nine years old and was yet holding to the promise of God that He would be given a child of promise. In the natural it was impossible - the barrier before Abraham was insurmountable. But a closer look at the Name and why it was given would make the believer see why this is his best weapon for bringing down barriers.

The Name means "The heavily breasted One". He who has more nourishing that His children would ever need.

God had revealed Himself by other Names to Abraham. For example Elohim which makes God known as the "One who preserves nature and its laws". Elohim presents God as the Awesome One deserving our worship. But El-Shaddai is the practical Name of God and by that Name it means

He is able to constrain nature and natural laws.

By His practical Name El-Shaddai, He is able to override natural laws, prolong things where it is said to be over, reverse laws where it says it cannot be changed, and accelerate laws which He created as Elohim to make things happen so fast.

By His Name El-Shaddai He can override any law which is contrary to the peace of His people.

God can reverse natural laws to fulfil things He promised to just one of His children. Abraham, ninety-nine years old; the law of nature says it is impossible for him to have a child, but understand that El-Shaddai makes you not to look at the circumstance, but to look at the practical ability of God, to look beyond the natural.

By His Name El-Shaddai, He makes things that seem impossible to turn around.

Jesus operated in this capacity when He turned water to wine in John 2:1-10.

And the third day there was a marriage in Cana of Galilee; and the mother of Jesus was there: And both Jesus was called, and his disciples, to the marriage. And when they wanted wine, the mother of Jesus saith unto him, They have no wine. Jesus saith unto her, Woman, what have I to do with thee? mine hour is not yet come. His mother saith unto the servants, Whatsoever he saith unto you, do it. And there were set there six waterpots of stone, after the manner of the purifying of the Jews, containing two or three firkins apiece. Jesus saith unto them, Fill the waterpots with water. And they filled them up to the brim. And he saith unto them, Draw out now, and bear unto the governor of the feast. And they bare it. When the ruler of the feast had tasted the water that was made wine, and knew not whence it was: (but the servants which drew the water knew;) the governor of the feast called the bridegroom, And saith unto him, Every man at the beginning doth set forth good wine; and when men have well drunk, then that which is worse: but thou hast kept the good wine until now.
John 2:1-10 (KJV)

The process which the wine given to the audience should have taken to reach vintage would be eight years. Sow the seed, grow the grape tree, harvest it, squeeze out the wine, and store it away to become vintage wine which is praised by the chairman. All this could probably take no less than eight years. But El-Shaddai by His practical Name, did what should take eight years in a few minutes.

When you need a barrier breaking experience, call on the Name of Jesus. Stop figuring out how the bills will be paid. It is a job for El-Shaddai. Stop figuring out how the barriers will come down. It is a job for El-Shaddai.

You are going to see God accelerate natural laws to get you out of a situation, to get you into your favour, to get you up when you are down, to get you there when they said it is too late.

The barrier breaker anointing that is in the Name El-Shaddai means that He is able to accelerate, override, and speed up the breakthrough as long as you hold on to your right to use that Name.

THE BLOOD OF JESUS

The Blood is the one scarlet thread that ties the sixty-six books of the Bible together.

Manifesting in Genesis, the blood kept speaking all through. Man's life depended on it.

For it is the life of all flesh; the blood of it is for the life thereof: therefore I said unto the children of Israel, Ye shall eat the blood of no manner of flesh: for the life of all flesh is the blood thereof: whosoever eateth it shall be cut off.
Leviticus 17:14 (KJV)

Man's redemption depended on it.

And almost all things are by the law purged with blood; and without shedding of blood is no remission.
Hebrews 9:22 (KJV)

His protection also from the angel of death depended on it.

And all the firstborn in the land of Egypt shall die, from the firstborn of Pharaoh that sitteth upon his throne, even unto the firstborn of the maidservant that is behind the mill; and all the firstborn of beasts.
Exodus 11:5 (KJV)

When Israel was confronted with death in Goshen, the instruction was to put the blood upon the doorpost.

And they shall take of the blood, and strike it on the two side posts and on the upper door post of the houses, wherein they shall eat it.
Exodus 12:7 (KJV)

It was so that a rejection of the gospel and of the message was regarded as trampling the blood of the Son of God underfoot.

He that despised Moses' law died without mercy under two or three witnesses: Of how much sorer punishment, suppose ye, shall he be thought worthy, who hath trodden under foot the Son of God, and hath counted the blood of the covenant, wherewith he was sanctified, an unholy thing, and hath done despite unto the Spirit of grace?
Hebrews 10:28-29 (KJV)

The blood became a sign for those people in a strange land, for their protection and their keeping.

And the blood shall be to you for a token upon the houses where ye are: and when I see the blood, I will pass over you, and the plague shall not be upon you to destroy you, when I smite the land of Egypt.

And ye shall take a bunch of hyssop, and dip it in the blood that is in the bason, and strike the lintel and the two side posts with the blood that is in the bason; and none of you shall go out at the door of his house until the morning.
Exodus 12:13, 22 (KJV)

If they were to be kept from harm, they were to stay under the blood.

...... and none of you shall go out at the door of his house until the morning.
Exodus 12:22b (KJV)

The Old Testament church accepted the blood as the basis for salvation and protection without question. If we must overcome satanic barriers, we must do the same. Walk by faith and not by sight.

> *For we walk by faith, not by sight:*
> *2 Corinthians 5:7 (KJV)*

Several scriptural instances indicate that the blood is the weapon against all kinds of barriers.

1. It is the blood for our justification.

> *Much more then, being now justified by his blood, we*
> *shall be saved from wrath through him.*
> *Romans 5:9 (KJV)*

2. It is the blood of our redemption bringing us out of the slave market of sin,

and the fetters the enemy meant to use to hold us down.

> *Forasmuch as ye know that ye were not redeemed with*
> *corruptible things, as silver and gold, from your vain*
> *conversation received by tradition from your fathers; But*
> *with the precious blood of Christ, as of a lamb without*
> *blemish and without spot:*
> *1 Peter 1:18-19 (KJV)*

3. It is the blood that makes peace with God and that brings the peace of God,

in the time of trouble and satanic depression.

That ye might walk worthy of the Lord unto all pleasing,
being fruitful in every good work, and increasing in the
knowledge of God;
Colossians 1:10 (KJV)

4. It is the blood that protects us and speaks on our behalf and declares us to be God's property.

Wherefore Jesus also, that he might sanctify the people
with his own blood, suffered without the gate.
Hebrews 13:12 (KJV)

5. It is the blood that brought our cleansing from every sin that Satan uses to condemn and hold us.

But if we walk in the light, as he is in the light, we have
fellowship one with another, and the blood of Jesus Christ
his Son cleanseth us from all sin.
1 John 1:7 (KJV)

If we confess our sins, he is faithful and just to forgive us
our sins, and to cleanse us from all unrighteousness.
1 John 1:9 (KJV)

6. It is the blood that speaks victory in the face of the worst adversity and satanic attack.

And they overcame him by the blood of the Lamb, and by the word of their testimony; and they loved not their lives unto the death.
Revelation 12:11 (KJV)

7. It is the blood that will bring back lost glory, lost possessions, and lost dominion.

What is man, that thou art mindful of him? and the son of man, that thou visitest him? For thou hast made him a little lower than the angels, and hast crowned him with glory and honour.
Psalms 8:4-5 (KJV)

8. It is the blood that speaks on your behalf and makes such a difference and marks you out, separate from the unsaved.

And there shall be a great cry throughout all the land of Egypt, such as there was none like it, nor shall be like it any more.   But against any of the children of Israel shall not a dog move his tongue, against man or beast: that ye may know how that the LORD doth put a difference between the Egyptians and Israel.
Exodus 11:6-7 (KJV)

9. It is the blood that will speak so strongly, break all barriers, and get all our stolen property and hindered properties restored.

And Pharaoh rose up in the night, he, and all his servants, and all the Egyptians; and there was a great cry in Egypt; for there was not a house where there was not one dead. And he called for Moses and Aaron by night, and said, Rise up, and get you forth from among my people, both ye and the children of Israel; and go, serve the LORD, as ye have said. Also take your flocks and your herds, as ye have said, and be gone; and bless me also.
Exodus 12:30-32 (KJV)

During the week of Christ's trial, death and resurrection, something most significant took place in the blood realm. Christ the Redeemer shed blood from five vantage points in His body. Each speaks of the barrier breaking power of the blood. Each speaks of the prophetic dimension of the blood.

The blood is meant to bring deliverance in five unique areas.

1. The hands of Christ were pierced, and that was for the regaining of our economic power.

Then delivered he him therefore unto them to be crucified. And they took Jesus, and led him away. And he bearing his cross went forth into a place called the place of a skull, which is called in the Hebrew Golgotha: Where they crucified him, and two other with him, on either side one, and Jesus in the midst.
John 19:16-18 (KJV)

The LORD shall command the blessing upon thee in thy storehouses, and in all that thou settest thine hand unto; and he shall bless thee in the land which the LORD thy God giveth thee. The LORD shall open unto thee his good treasure, the heaven to give the rain unto thy land in his season, and to bless all the work of thine hand: and thou shalt lend unto many nations, and thou shalt not borrow.
Deuteronomy 28:8,12 (KJV)

2. When on the cross His feet were put together and pierced with the nail. This speaks of regaining dominion; having put everything under His feet.

And the LORD God said unto the serpent, Because thou hast done this, thou art cursed above all cattle, and above every beast of the field; upon thy belly shalt thou go, and dust shalt thou eat all the days of thy life:
And I will put enmity between thee and the woman, and between thy seed and her seed; it shall bruise thy head, and thou shalt bruise his heel.
Genesis 3:14-15 (KJV)

Forasmuch then as the children are partakers of flesh and blood, he also himself likewise took part of the same; that through death he might destroy him that had the power of death, that is, the devil; And deliver them who through fear of death were all their lifetime subject to bondage.
Hebrews 2:14-15 (KJV)

Which he wrought in Christ, when he raised him from the dead, and set him at his own right hand in the heavenly places, Far above all principality, and power, and might, and dominion, and every name that is named, not only in this world, but also in that which is to come: And hath put all things under his feet, and gave him to be the head over all things to the church,
Ephesians 1:20-22 (KJV)

3. At the whipping post thirty-nine stripes were laid on Him. The lacerations and the brokenness of His body poured out the blood. That prophetic action was for the healing and health of the believer. Every sickness; physical, emotional, spiritual and psychosomatic has been paid for by that action.

Then Pilate therefore took Jesus, and scourged him.
John 19:1 (KJV)

Surely he hath borne our griefs, and carried our sorrows: yet we did esteem him stricken, smitten of God, and afflicted. But he was wounded for our transgressions, he was bruised for our iniquities: the chastisement of our peace was upon him; and with his stripes we are healed.
Isaiah 53:4-5 (KJV)

4. They pushed a crown of thorns on the head of the Saviour, and as the blood poured down, it brought a release from every curse.

Christ hath redeemed us from the curse of the law, being made a curse for us: for it is written, Cursed is every one that hangeth on a tree: That the blessing of Abraham might come on the Gentiles through Jesus Christ; that we might receive the promise of the Spirit through faith.
Galatians 3:13-14 (KJV)

Then the soldiers of the governor took Jesus into the common hall, and gathered unto him the whole band of soldiers. And they stripped him, and put on him a scarlet robe. And when they had platted a crown of thorns, they put it upon his head, and a reed in his right hand: and they bowed the knee before him, and mocked him, saying, Hail, King of the Jews! And they spit upon him, and took the reed, and smote him on the head. And after that they had mocked him, they took the robe off from him, and put his own raiment on him, and led him away to crucify him.
Matthew 27:27-31 (KJV)

The placing of the crown of thorns upon His head causing blood to pour out and break the power of the curse, also meant a restoration to a place of authority and dominion.

Every barrier that has stolen your dominion over life is broken as the blood is applied.

For we have not an high priest which cannot be touched with the feeling of our infirmities; but was in all points tempted like as we are, yet without sin. Let us therefore come boldly unto the throne of grace, that we may obtain mercy, and find grace to help in time of need.
Hebrews 4:15-16 (KJV)

5. John 19:32-35 indicates that His side was pierced, and His blood mingled with water poured out. The outpouring speaks of a flow.

"There is a fountain filled with blood drawn from Emmanuel's vein, it still cleanses, it still speaks, it still sets free, it still satisfies".

The believer may today plead that blood as his protection and guarantee from the barriers of sin. The blood from His side also speaks of love - it being close to His heart. Whenever we plead the blood, we touch the heart of the One who shed it for us, and every barrier releases us from its grip.

It is the blood that purchased us and turned us to God's Property.

Ye are bought with a price; be not ye the servants of men.
1 Corinthians 7:23 (KJV)

For ye are bought with a price: therefore glorify God in your body, and in your spirit, which are God's.
1 Corinthians 6:20 (KJV)

....But with the precious blood of Christ, as of a lamb without blemish and without spot:
1 Peter 1:19 (KJV)

It is the weapon for disarming principalities and powers, disannuling their ability and gaining victory over them.

And having spoiled principalities and powers, he made a shew of them openly, triumphing over them in it.
Colossians 2:15 (KJV)

And, having made peace through the blood of his cross, by him to reconcile all things unto himself; by him, I say, whether they be things in earth, or things in heaven.
Colossians 1:20 (KJV)

The blood is your source for gaining approval from God and favour from His throne.

For he hath made him to be sin for us, who knew no sin; that we might be made the righteousness of God in him.
2 Corinthians 5:21 (KJV)

To shut every satanic door, or open the doors of favour, the blood will be there to speak for you.

Be ye angry, and sin not: let not the sun go down upon your wrath: Neither give place to the devil.
Ephesians 4:26-27 (KJV)

It can shut the door of strife, and all the ones the enemy opens to take advantage of you.

Lastly,
it is a speaking blood.

It is a blood that cries out for your healing and deliverance. The blood of Abel called for vengeance, but the blood of Jesus speaks better things.

And to Jesus the mediator of the new covenant, and to the blood of sprinkling, that speaketh better things than that of Abel.
Hebrews 12:24 (KJV)

The blood is still speaking today; it is pleading for your victory in the presence of the Father.

Many have argued about pleading the blood. The word plead, *reed* in the Hebrew means *to strive, contend, or to conduct a legal battle*. If pleading is conducting a legal battle, you certainly must do so, because Satan has no other answer to the weapon called the blood. He has nothing to stand the devastating power contained in it.

It spoke for a prostitute and moved her to become a woman in the lineage of Jesus.

By faith the harlot Rahab perished not with them that believed not, when she had received the spies with peace.
Hebrews 11:31 (KJV)

When the enemy shall come in like a flood, raise the standard of the blood - that establishes and guarantees your victory.

BOLDNESS: THE BARRIER BREAKER'S MANTLE

The adversary uses intimidation to limit the believer, magnify mountains, belittle the anointing that we carry, and try to keep us from maximising what belongs to us.

The enemy knows that once you are without boldness, you are also without the ability to stand and win.

Victory for the believer must be to fight until you possess what God has already promised. To go into the enemy's camp and take what belongs to you.

WHAT IS BOLDNESS?

Boldness comes from the Greek word *Parrhess*, it means *outspoken, frankness, bluntness, assurance, confidence, being free*, and *being plain*.

Another Greek word *Tharrew* gives boldness the meaning of *extreme conduct, to be venturesome, to be courageous, to dare*.

OUTSPOKENNESS

This is the grace and ability to speak boldly and confidently as God gives the grace.

Let your conversation be without covetousness; and be content with such things as ye have: for he hath said, I will never leave thee, nor forsake thee. So that we may boldly say, The Lord is my helper, and I will not fear what man shall do unto me.
Hebrews 13:5-6 (KJV)

It is boldly saying what the Word of God says concerning you; declaring the end of a matter, even at the beginning of it.

Jesus operated in the anointing of boldness.
One time King Herod sent his cohorts to Jesus to intimidate Him and probably limit the scope of His ministry by saying that Herod was after His life. Jesus' response was very simple *"Go ye and tell that fox, behold I cast out devils"*.

If he meant that his words would scare Jesus, it did nothing of such. Jesus was not moved by the intimidation from the pit of hell. This kind of boldness makes a child of God to be able to speak knowing that hell cannot respond when you are backed by the Word of God.

We see another example of Jesus in John 7:26.

But, lo, he speaketh boldly, and they say nothing unto him. Do the rulers know indeed that this is the very Christ?
John 7:26 (KJV)

Boldness of speech is necessary because with your mouth confession is made unto salvation.

That if thou shalt confess with thy mouth the Lord Jesus, and shalt believe in thine heart that God hath raised him from the dead, thou shalt be saved.
Romans 10:9 (KJV)

You must boldly declare what God says concerning you and turn your mouth to become the source of life.

The mouth of a righteous man is a well of life: but violence covereth the mouth of the wicked.
Proverbs 10:11 (KJV)

The apostles operated under the mantle of boldness to speak.

Long time therefore abode they speaking boldly in the Lord, which gave testimony unto the word of his grace, and granted signs and wonders to be done by their hands.
Acts 14:3 (KJV)

They spoke boldly and God guaranteed that the words of His servants were backed with signs and wonders, none of them fell and died.

Today God is saying.

I am the LORD thy God, which brought thee out of the land of Egypt: open thy mouth wide, and I will fill it.
Psalms 81:10 (KJV)

Boldness of speech is not mere noise. You are either a noisemaker or a voice for a change in the things of the Spirit.

When you speak as a voice backed by an anointing that destroys yokes, you would rebuke the enemy and he would not be able to stand, but flee.

ASSURANCE

Boldness is also assurance.
It is knowing in your 'knower' that the God who spoke the Word still backs it with all the resources of heaven and earth. He will supply what His

Word promises, He will make a way where He said He will, He will do just what He said.

Paul wrote to a young pastor Timothy and in doing so gave him a calm assurance.

> *For the which cause I also suffer these things:*
> *nevertheless I am not ashamed: for I know whom I have*
> *believed, and am persuaded that he is able to keep that*
> *which I have committed unto him against that day.*
> *2 Timothy 1:12 (KJV)*

Boldness is informed by persuasion.

You can only be bold in the area where you have a conviction. Until you are persuaded about healing, you cannot boldly receive the grace of healing. If you must operate and receive all that God has promised for your loved ones to be saved, you must be persuaded.

CONFIDENCE

Confidence is being free; it is plainness without arrogance, it is demonstrating the power of the gospel without necessarily showing off.

Boldness expressed in confidence protects you from falling into the traps the enemy sets.

For the LORD shall be thy confidence, and shall keep thy foot from being taken.
Proverbs 3:26 (KJV)

Confidence is what you have when you refuse to have a plan B, but trust totally in the promises of God.

It is better to trust in the LORD than to put confidence in man.
Psalms 118:8 (KJV)

Confidence is your strength for overcoming.

It is the sense of serenity and peace you know and experience in the face of the greatest adversity, but with a calm assurance that what God said would come to pass.

For thus saith the Lord GOD, the Holy One of Israel; In returning and rest shall ye be saved; in quietness and in confidence shall be your strength: and ye would not.
Isaiah 30:15 (KJV)

Confidence is required when prayer is offered.

It is knowing that because you do not have a manifestation now does not mean it shall not come to pass. The boldness that is expressed in confidence makes us to go to bed and not have to carry on our shoulders the burden we have placed upon the Lord.

And this is the confidence that we have in him, that, if we ask any thing according to his will, he heareth us:
1 John 5:14 (KJV)

Confidence would not falter, fail or seek alternatives when it is faced with opposition.

Godly confidence would not tremble before Herod, Goliath, or whatever problem.

Confidence informed Elijah's action when he challenged the widow to cook the last meal, knowing that even in the face of famine, drought and lack, the supply would still come.

Confidence informed the action of Hezekiah when he blatantly refused to bow to the demand of the king of Assyria, though he was the king of only two tribes.

Be strong and courageous, be not afraid nor dismayed for the king of Assyria, nor for all the multitude that is with him: for there be more with us than with him: With him is an arm of flesh; but with us is the LORD our God to help us, and to fight our battles. And the people rested themselves upon the words of Hezekiah king of Judah.
2 Chronicles 32:7-8 (KJV)

Confidence assures your access to God's presence.

Confidence delivers to you a great reward. While cowards die before the battle, the confident believer will tear down the barriers and remove the burdens. Do not listen to the howling voice of a thousand demons that try to gain your attention, attacking your mind, wanting you to take your eye off the Lord.

Be bold to know that if God said it, then it stands, you must win.

COURAGE

There is a dimension to boldness that is the exercise of courage.

The Greek word suggests an extreme conduct carried out by the leading of the Holy Spirit. It is being adventurous without walking in the flesh. It is being daring, treading where angels dread by reason of the Holy Spirit, to possess what God has earmarked for you.

If the three Hebrew men had compromised and not taken a courageous stand they would not have defied an ungodly king.

Courage is necessary to assert your dominion on earth. The difference between the believer who knows about dominion and the one who walks in it, is the ability to exercise courage.

Courage was what informed Nehemiah's ability to rebuild the walls of Jericho.

With enemies within and without, and those who had neglected the Word of God now mocking Him for taking a stand to see progress, Nehemiah was able to focus his eye and that of God's people on the reason for their exploits.

And I looked, and rose up, and said unto the nobles, and to the rulers, and to the rest of the people, Be not ye afraid of them: remember the Lord, which is great and terrible, and fight for your brethren, your sons, and your daughters, your wives, and your houses.
Nehemiah 4:14 (KJV)

Run to the battle, run to the spoil and possess your possessions.

WHY BOLDNESS?

Boldness determines the sphere of your ruling in life.

It determines if you will continue as a slave of circumstance or a dominator over the elements of life. Boldness determines if Christ is magnified through your life, or if you are just one more of the many who crowd humanity and make no impact.

According to my earnest expectation and my hope, that in nothing I shall be ashamed, but that with all boldness, as always, so now also Christ shall be magnified in my body, whether it be by life, or by death.
Philippians 1:20 (KJV)

How many people have lost opportunities and lost favours.

How many have turned their back with their tail between their legs because the enemy intimidated them.

It is boldness in Christ that marks you out and causes you to demonstrate abilities beyond your natural person.

Boldness in Christ will make you stand out, so people do not step on you and walk all over you. When you operate in holy boldness, it will mark you out, and make your gift and calling to come forth so that you are a blessing to your generation.

Those who have found their confidence in God, end their lives glorifying Him.

*For if I have boasted any thing to him of you, I am not
ashamed; but as we spake all things to you in truth,
even so our boasting, which I made before Titus, is
found a truth.*
2 Corinthians 7:14 (KJV)

You need boldness, because when you face satanic
threats, obvious dangers and opposition to your
faith, the assuring thing you will do when you are
bold is to proclaim God's Word and stand on it
until it is fulfilled.

*And now, Lord, behold their threatenings: and grant unto
thy servants, that with all boldness they may speak thy
word,*
Acts 4:29 (KJV)

The countenance of a man who is
full of boldness, brightens up
because he knows something the
enemy does not know - that he
would win at last. Boldness helps to
take charge and declare an intended
end to the situation.

*Who is as the wise man? and who knoweth the
interpretation of a thing? a man's wisdom maketh his face
to shine, and the boldness of his face shall be changed.*
Ecclesiastes 8:1 (KJV)

In the book of Zechariah, Zerubbabel declares an intended end to the mountain, even though it seemed to be daunting.

> *Who art thou, O great mountain? before Zerubbabel thou shalt become a plain: and he shall bring forth the headstone thereof with shoutings, crying, Grace, grace unto it.*
> *Zecheriah 4:7 (KJV)*

Boldness as given by the Holy Spirit is the key to overcoming an inferiority complex.

Our advancement as a society has not taken away the complexities of life but rather has increased it. Man's inhumanity to man has taken away people's sense of confidence and assurance.

When you receive Holy Ghost boldness, you know who you are in God.

So if Satan wants you to think less of who you are, feel less and receive less, you are able to boldly declare that you are chosen by God, and ordained by Him to live and enjoy abundant life.

The thief cometh not, but for to steal, and to kill, and to destroy: I am come that they might have life, and that they might have it more abundantly.
John 10:10 (KJV)

Any ministry that will make impact is likely to be confronted by opposers who want such to become silent.

Boldness as given by the Holy Spirit fires you up and makes your ministry a proof-producing enterprise.

Now when they saw the boldness of Peter and John, and perceived that they were unlearned and ignorant men, they marvelled; and they took knowledge of them, that they had been with Jesus. And beholding the man which was healed standing with them, they could say nothing against it.
Acts 4:13-14 (KJV)

Brethren we need boldness today. It is our greatest strategy if we must expose how spineless the enemy is.

Goliath knew the power of fear, he said things to paralyse Israel and make them frozen on the spot, until David showed up on the horizon. My dear friend you need boldness because that is what will introduce you to the best days that are ahead of you.

You need boldness; everyone who has made a mark in Bible times were known for their outstanding boldness.

They refused to go with the flow; rather they flowed contrary to how everyone flows. The difference between a living fish and a dead one is that sometimes a living fish will flow and swim against the flow of the river, whilst a dead fish is carried away in the direction of the river's flow.

Boldness marks you out and makes you operate differently from the predictable.

Boldness of course requires a sound mind, because a broken man would have a broken heart, and a broken person is a defeated person.

David expresses his confidence in God and a bold assurance that informed why he took on the lion, the bear, and finally Goliath.

Yea, though I walk through the valley of the shadow of death, I will fear no evil: for thou art with me; thy rod and thy staff they comfort me.
Psalms 23:4 (KJV)

His confidence was not in man, if it were in man he would have been put to shame.

Thus saith the LORD; Cursed be the man that trusteth in man, and maketh flesh his arm, and whose heart departeth from the LORD.
Jeremiah 17:5 (KJV)

If you are still asking the question why you need Holy Spirit boldness, it is simply put. It is your number one requirement for doing greater exploits in these last days, your number one requirement to preach the good news of Jesus Christ in the face of opposition and ridicule. It is the mantle that must rest on you if you must go in and take your possession.

These are the days when Christians should take territories, do signs, and do wonders. It would only be possible in the atmosphere where the barrier breaker anointing of boldness rests upon your life.

Brethren its time to scale heights, and to reach levels we have never reached.

EXAMPLES OF BOLDNESS

Wherefore seeing we also are compassed about with so great a cloud of witnesses, let us lay aside every weight, and the sin which doth so easily beset us, and let us run with patience the race that is set before us,
Looking unto Jesus the author and finisher of our faith; who for the joy that was set before him endured the cross, despising the shame, and is set down at the right hand of the throne of God.
Hebrews 12:1-2 (KJV)

We are surrounded by men of faith who did great exploits, but they would not have joined the hall of faith if they did not act in boldness. It takes boldness to flow against the stream. It took boldness for Abraham, who was over ninety to declare that he would have a child.

Boldness made Moses to reject the riches of Egypt and choose to suffer persecution with the people of God because He had an expectation.

JESUS

If anyone stands out as an example of boldness it will be the Lord Jesus Christ. His teaching was with authority, it was different.

And they were amazed at His teaching, for His word was
with authority and ability and weight and power.
Luke 4:32 (Amplified)

Jesus demonstrated authority, ability, weight and power in His words. And if He did, by reason of boldly entering and taking what belongs to us, we are told that "Just as He is, so are we".

Herein is our love made perfect, that we may have
boldness in the day of judgment: because as he is, so are
we in this world.
1 John 4:17 (KJV)

If "as He is, so are we", how did Jesus act boldly when He was on earth? He commanded demons to leave with authority and power, and they obeyed. He spoke peace to nature like it had ears. He did not spend time studying the storms before commanding its rage to stop.

His boldness helped Him to establish His position of authority on earth, and the One who did all this spoke to us in Matthew 28:20, giving us the assurance that we should go with His power, we should go with His presence, and we will be backed by His anointing.

Teaching them to observe all things whatsoever I have commanded you: and, lo, I am with you alway, even unto the end of the world. Amen.
Matthew 28:20 (KJV)

DAVID

David broke the mould of obscurity, when as a shepherd he took on a lion one-on-one, and a grizzly bear one-on-one. Unknown to him he was being prepared for a showdown with Goliath. Every trouble is intended to introduce us to our favoured day, our breakthrough, and our testimony. Never let a problem leave you as it met you.

Goliath's voice had sent fear into the camp of Israel, their confidence shattered, their boldness gone. Who knows they probably boasted before the battle came, but when Goliath spoke the words that sent fear to their heart, they could not lift their finger or raise their voice. They were shattered as an army that could not shoot a bullet.

But into this scenario came David. David's confidence was in the fact that God had done it before, and He would do it again. If God begins a good work, He never leaves it unfinished.

Boldness is your key to rise from one rung of the ladder to another rung of the ladder.

The battle you face today is intended to introduce you to your testimony.

If you have no 'tests' you would know no 'testimony', if you have no 'tries' you would not know 'triumph'. You only possess these things by reason of boldness.

David manifested his boldness by not walking, but running to the giants.

RECEIVING THE GRACE OF BOLDNESS

The barrier breaker's anointing rides on the crest of boldness.

But boldness is expressed by actions or words that are spoken. Start today by speaking God's intention to the situation instead of describing the situation.

Jesus never described a problem, He spoke to it. He did not describe the state of the condition of the fig tree. When He was told there was no fruit on it, He spoke His intention; *"May you not bear fruit"*.

He did not spend time analysing the food shortage or calling experts on how to supply food to five thousand people.

He spoke it to manifestation. That is the Christ we are instructed to imitate.

It is important to walk in the reality of the power of God's Word; in the reality of the gospel of Jesus Christ. Because it is while you speak faith words and act out faith words that boldness is seen and result follows.

Manifest this boldness in your prayer.

Let us therefore come boldly unto the throne of grace, that we may obtain mercy, and find grace to help in time of need.
Hebrews 4:16 (KJV)

When you come against sickness and disease just do what Jesus said to do, and He will play His own part.

Now when they saw the boldness of Peter and John, and perceived that they were unlearned and ignorant men, they marvelled; and they took knowledge of them, that they had been with Jesus.
Acts 4:13 (KJV)

There may be a threat to your life. Your response should not be to the threat, but rather declare the Word of God.

And now, Lord, behold their threatenings: and grant unto thy servants, that with all boldness they may speak thy word. And when they had prayed, the place was shaken where they were assembled together; and they were all filled with the Holy Ghost, and they spake the word of God with boldness.
Acts 4:29, 31 (KJV)

When the powers that be tried to silence the apostles, their only desire was for the boldness to keep declaring what God said, and not carry out what man wanted. When you seem to be surrounded by an unspeakable darkness, remember God's Word and declare that you will not be afraid, no matter what man does to you.

Yea, though I walk through the valley of the shadow of death, I will fear no evil: for thou art with me; thy rod and thy staff they comfort me.
Psalms 23:4 (KJV)

Let the assurance of His presence
see you through any challenging
times, and by reason of boldness
come to His throne.

Come boldly like a lion because you are an
offspring of the lion of Judah.

The wicked flee when no man pursueth: but the righteous
are bold as a lion.
Proverbs 28:1 (KJV)

Open your mouth wide from today,
so that every mystery of the gospel
will be confirmed as you boldly
declare what God said He can do
and will do.

When someone is waiting to see you fail, thank
God for His Word that cannot lie.

So that we may boldly say, The Lord is my helper, and I
will not fear what man shall do unto me.
Hebrews 13:6 (KJV)

Know this for sure my friend that your victory is a
foregone conclusion. If God said it, that is good
enough, it will come to pass. Confidence and

boldness will begin to produce an unspeakable reward. It will begin to recompense you for everything you have lost.

And many of the brethren in the Lord, waxing confident by my bonds, are much more bold to speak the word without fear.
Philippians 1:14 (KJV)

Boldness will back you up and take you into the realms of breakthrough you have never imagined before.

Cast not away therefore your confidence, which hath great recompence of reward.
Hebrews 10:35 (KJV)

In conclusion my dear friend, what are you waiting for? The Lord has given you a land of good things. It is time to press in and make them yours. He tells us that great signs and wonders will follow those who believe.

Boldness demands that you go today and lay those hands of yours on some circumstances and begin to see a change.

Three times He said in Mark 11:23, 24 to speak to the mountains. Speak boldly to that mountain today, and act as if it is done, results will follow.

For verily I say unto you, That whosoever shall say unto this mountain, Be thou removed, and be thou cast into the sea; and shall not doubt in his heart, but shall believe that those things which he saith shall come to pass; he shall have whatsoever he saith. Therefore I say unto you, What things soever ye desire, when ye pray, believe that ye receive them, and ye shall have them.
Mark 11:23-24 (KJV)

Many do not get their breakthrough because they are playing safe. You are not safe if you play safe.

Only stand on the Word of God, not your feelings and not the facts you see. Facts and truth are not the same. It may be a fact that you have a certain ailment, your finances are not going well, and you have had difficulties in your marriage. It is not the truth that it is too late or you cannot overcome. As long as you hold onto God's Word and confront the mountain with confidence you will see a divine turnaround.

Your confidence in God must be demonstrated, that is where your strength lies.

For thus saith the Lord GOD, the Holy One of Israel; In returning and rest shall ye be saved; in quietness and in confidence shall be your strength: and ye would not.
Isaiah 30:15 (KJV)

And whatever you hear, feel or see, know that the Word of God works mightily in you and you must finish your course with a total testimony.

But none of these things move me, neither count I my life dear unto myself, so that I might finish my course with joy, and the ministry, which I have received of the Lord Jesus, to testify the gospel of the grace of God.
Acts 20:24 (KJV)

CHAPTER THREE

BREAKING LIFE'S BARRIERS

Have you ever heard people say life is not always fair, or the ones who would say, "Why do bad things happen to people?" or as in the case of people who were born with certain limitations, challenges or battles. Some cannot handle it and therefore they ask the question, "Why do humans suffer this much, particularly the children?" "What did they do to deserve it?"

These questions are deep, philosophical, and yet logical. The quest for an answer to such questions of life have made some people yield themselves to be manipulated, abused, used, and pushed around. The absence of answers has made some people to either look or search until they find the appropriate answer, turning impossible situations to possible ones, and using the battles they face as stepping stones to the future.

The majority though do not do that, rather the questions they cannot answer, and the battles and the challenges they face have become the breeding ground of things that tend to stop them; limitations, failures of the past, people's opinion, personal insecurities, self esteem problems, bad teaching from those who raised them and bad parenting. The list could go on.

To top that is the case of people who from birth had certain physical disabilities.

This feeling is summarised by a statement I saw written on a wall in a public bus garage in Africa, "Man was born to suffer". That to me is not the conclusion of an African under the scorching sun, it would be the same in the Amazon jungle or among the Eskimos of Alaska.

What has the bible got to say? The Scriptures do not take us away from the arena of battle. Take a trip from Genesis to Revelation, you will find that the principle and pattern of God is always to bring out a miracle from a mess; to turn a battle to a place where He will bless His people. We face these things from a Scriptural point of view, sometimes because we are not yet the persons God wants us to be, and these things become our refining fire.

Battle from a bible point of view, seems like one of the legitimate ways to become God's property. Did not Job say *"When He has tried me, I shall come forth as gold"*(something to be cherished). So we go through these battles because there is a master plan at the end of it, and the One whom we serve calls Himself "The Captain of our salvation".

With this truth in mind, let us observe a bible character in whose life we see three major barriers which are a replica of the things we may be going through also. To me these three barriers are the key ones to be broken for a man to make sense of his destiny.

And they came to Jericho: and as he went out of Jericho with his disciples and a great number of people, blind Bartimaeus, the son of Timaeus, sat by the highway side begging. And when he heard that it was Jesus of Nazareth, he began to cry out, and say, Jesus, thou Son of David, have mercy on me. And many charged him that he should hold his peace: but he cried the more a great deal, Thou Son of David, have mercy on me. And Jesus stood still, and commanded him to be called. And they call the blind man, saying unto him, Be of good comfort, rise; he calleth thee. And he, casting away his garment, rose, and came to Jesus. And Jesus answered and said unto him, What wilt thou that I should do unto thee? The blind man said unto him, Lord, that I might receive my sight. And Jesus said unto him, Go thy way; thy faith hath made thee whole. And immediately he received his sight, and followed Jesus in the way.
Mark 10:46-52 (KJV)

The three synoptic gospels record the account of Bartimaeus' healing, and though his name was not mentioned in two, it is clear from the background. We have no indication that he was born blind, but it can be inferred that it was his experience from childhood.

THE BLINDNESS BARRIER

Bartimaeus' condition meant that he could not appreciate colour but could only follow the sound he heard. Blindness is certainly a major challenge. Imagine what it is like and how dark the world is with your eyes closed for just one hour, and you trying to make your way around. Yet a greater challenge is spiritual blindness, and the blindness that is by reason of the lack of vision for life.

The absence of vision is a major challenge, because the picture you see determines a lot about your future.

I will stand upon my watch, and set me upon the tower, and will watch to see what he will say unto me, and what I shall answer when I am reproved.
Habakkuk 2:1 (KJV)

"The Law of Sight"

"Your destiny will be shaped by the vision in your heart. What you see in your spirit is what you get in material reality."

We have given this subject an exhaustive treatment in Breaking Barriers (Volume One). Yet it is important that we touch on it again, because the vision you see matters.

That is why you must never put before you what you do not want inside you.

The vision you see determines what you become, the picture you see provokes a reaction of blessing or cursing. The picture you see determines if you would be a failure or a success. The picture you see inspires what you pursue.

And, behold, a woman, which was diseased with an issue of blood twelve years, came behind him, and touched the hem of his garment: For she said within herself, If I may but touch his garment, I shall be whole. But Jesus turned him about, and when he saw her, he said, Daughter, be of good comfort; thy faith hath made thee whole. And the woman was made whole from that hour.
Matthew 9:20-22 (KJV)

The Scriptures make us to understand that the woman saw the Lord Jesus and pursued Him until she touched Him and became healed. God inspired Israel by painting a picture of the land which they were going to. The haemorrhaging woman saw a picture of her healing, and it released health in her body, because she said to herself "If I touch the hem of His garment, I shall be made whole". She saw herself in the future. When you see a picture of supply, it unlocks your faith to prosper.

What you see unlocks your faith and helps you in moments of difficulty.

Looking unto Jesus the author and finisher of our faith; who for the joy that was set before him endured the cross, despising the shame, and is set down at the right hand of the throne of God.
Hebrews 12:2 (KJV)

If the picture you see is wrong, the emotion you will express will be negative.

You cannot put before you a picture of those who offend your spirit, and be motivated to walk in love.

What you see provokes what you desire. Your vision determines your craving.

The picture you see determines the actions you take. A man who perpetually sees those who are succeeding around him, will desire to rise to the level of what he sees.

Israel saw itself as an inferior nation.

But the men that went up with him said, We be not able to go up against the people; for they are stronger than we. And they brought up an evil report of the land which they had searched unto the children of Israel, saying, The land, through which we have gone to search it, is a land that eateth up the inhabitants thereof; and all the people that we saw in it are men of a great stature. And there we saw the giants, the sons of Anak, which come of the giants: and we were in our own sight as grasshoppers, and so we were in their sight.
Numbers 13:31-33 (KJV)

They painted a picture of a defeated people, and every adult who participated in such imagery did not make it to the Promised Land. They embraced what they saw; they believed it, spoke it, imagined it and experienced it. They saw giants instead of God.

The picture you see determines the conquest you experience or the defeat you go through.

If your vision is wrong, you do not need another enemy, you become your own worse enemy.

On the other hand, no vision means no future, no direction, no breakthrough, and finally no testimony.

Natural blindness is a major barrier, but many have been able, in spite of such a disability, to make progress, but progress is impossible where it is a blindness of your life's vision.

SPIRITUAL BLINDNESS

Without vision there is no going, without the vision there is no destination. A journey undefined becomes a destination unreached.

In my opinion the single greatest barrier in life is to have no defined vision for yourself.

Where you have no clearly defined vision, you would find that life is like a rapidly rushing river. If you do not make a decision, the river would make one for you.

If you have no clear vision for yourself, people will define your life for you, and determine your actions and reactions for you.

Bartimaeus was also confronted with The Bondage Barrier.

THE BONDAGE BARRIER

And he, casting away his garment, rose, and came to Jesus.
Mark 10:50 (KJV)

When this man who had fought with blindness was finally given his invitation by Jesus, he found his speed limited by the garment which he wore. A Jewish garment for a man with a disability like himself was certainly a handful.

People were defined and given certain clothes to wear in Israel. Having been stripped of his pride and confidence as a man with such a disability, this garment was probably how he hid himself. It was a symbol of his bondage to self-pity.

A bondage is anything that tries to slow you down. It is often spiritual and psychological.

It cannot be seen, but it can be felt by people who are around a man who is experiencing bondage. In the case of Bartimaeus, it was probably that he was caught in the gall of depression. Israel was when it faced the battle of evil report.

And all the congregation lifted up their voice, and cried; and the people wept that night.
Numbers 14:1 (KJV)

The bondage barrier could also have come from a complaining spirit.

And all the children of Israel murmured against Moses and against Aaron: and the whole congregation said unto them, Would God that we had died in the land of Egypt! or would God we had died in this wilderness!
Numbers 14:2 (KJV)

Like Israel, Bartimaeus could have complained or asked the question, "Why me?" Why, is a question people ask oftentimes, but they fail to realise that, while God does not use the devil's tools to achieve His purpose, yet He is able to bring forth good out of what you are asking why about. Bartimaeus also possibly may have considered suicide, like Israel also did.

And all the children of Israel murmured against Moses and against Aaron: and the whole congregation said unto them, Would God that we had died in the land of Egypt! or would God we had died in this wilderness! And wherefore hath the LORD brought us unto this land, to fall by the sword, that our wives and our children should be a prey? were it not better for us to return into Egypt?
Numbers 14:2-3 (KJV)

In the pressure cooker world in which we live, suicide tendencies seem to rise every day. Suicide is particularly popular now among teenagers and people with failed businesses. Anyone's life, by committing suicide, does not mean the end of the matter, it is rather a complication of it. Because, if man must appear before God to answer for the life he has lived, to commit suicide is to take a precious life; in this case your own.

Imagine holding onto the rags that made up what was called his garment. Shivering in the shadows and believing there was no hope for him. Imagine

Bartimaeus wandering from town to town and village to village asking for pennies. Hanging around at street corners and sometimes having insensitive children picking on him and calling him names, knowing also that every movement he made was dependent on other people's good will.

Imagine the spirits that drove him about, the complaining, the depressive, and the suicidal spirits. And think of the fact that they all kept him in bondage, so that along with the pain of blindness in bible times when he could not have had a guide dog, a Braille book to read, a walking stick or a school for the blind, he certainly was in bondage.

But nothing could be more complicated than to be called Bartimaeus, the son of Timaeus. Because Bartimaeus really means the son of Timaeus. In effect his name was the son of Timaeus, the son of Timaeus. Bartimaeus, the son of Timaeus. Technically, he had no name. They only described him by his father's name.

There is nothing more painful than to be described by your problem. 'The man who was born blind'.

It is also safe to conclude that he had no address, no future, and no family. This would grab a man and hold him in the gall of depression.

Was Bartimaeus a man who felt loved? It is safe to conclude that Bartimaeus was surrounded by fears and physical problems; he experienced people's verbal abuse, possible physical abuse, and being robbed by miscreants.

There are bondages of all kinds, people who have suffered sexual abuse in the hand of those who took advantage of their innocence. The highest level of sexual abuse takes place within circles of intimacy; cousins, uncles, blended relationships; stepfathers and stepmothers.

In most cases it cannot be spoken out, it is considered a taboo, and if the people who had suffered spoke, nobody would believe them.

Bondages vary; there is peer rejection, marriage rejection, an unfaithful spouse who would not talk, or show friendship or love, and rejects you for who you are. That is bondage.

People carry rejection around like a smelly bag.

It caused the first murder when Cain sacrificed his brother, having been rejected by God.

People who suffer from the bondage of rejection, either for the wrong they have done or otherwise, react in different ways. For Potiphar's wife, she turned around and falsely accused, and caused the incarceration of Joseph.

Some people who have been rejected become dedicated critics of their peers and their leaders, because they have a personal sense of rejection. A critical spirit is evidence of a condemned rejected person.

Rejection retards and paralyses progress completely, because where a person who suffers from rejection is given true love, they would not believe that it is real and genuine.

Rejection would make a man fearful and stop taking risks because he is afraid of falling, and so he parks his life at the bus stop called "Stay Put".

It is in the midst of all this that Bartimaeus heard his name and threw the garment away. The last of Bartimaeus' barriers was a beggar's mentality.

A BEGGAR'S MENTALITY

Remember that Bartimaeus had been on the street all his life. He knew the street creed and had developed a hustler's mentality.

The absence of vision is devastating, the bondage barrier is limiting, but there probably is nothing worse than being held down by a beggar's mentality.

A man who has a beggar's mentality could be born again, living in the House of Bread, and still believes he does not deserve or qualify to receive anything from God. Instead of Scriptures like 2 Peter 1:4

Whereby are given unto us exceeding great and precious promises: that by these ye might be partakers of the divine nature, having escaped the corruption that is in the world through lust.
2 Peter 1:4 (KJV)

A man with a beggar's mentality would rather say: "I'm trapped, I'm dressed for begging, that's what fits me.

"This blessing is too good for me".
Sometimes it is not said, but the attitude suggests,
"Some blessings are too good for me"
"I cannot stand being blessed"
"Things only work for others"
"We're not called to succeed, we're only called to be faithful", as if success is a taboo for the believer.

The beggar's mentality limits personal aspirations and desires. The beggar's mentality limits one's prayers. The beggar's mentality creates the innate belief that "what would be, would be".

The beggar's mentality makes one to continue to be a hustler, even though he is now a prince of God. A beggar's mentality would twist Scriptures, that have to do with blessing and favour, belittle the impact and misinterpret what it says. For example the Scriptures says,

The rich and poor meet together: the LORD is the maker of them all.
Proverbs 22:2 (KJV)

The man with the beggar's mentality will misinterpret the Scripture, which says, "Godliness with contentment is great gain" and make it look like "Godliness with containment is great gain".

You cannot receive what you do not know belongs to you.

Biblical ignorance is at the root of poverty for most believers. If God's Word says you will be blessed and highly favoured, prosperous and succeeding and you are not, your belief system is either wrong, or you are missing certain elements that would make all come together.

Certainly misquoting Scriptures and the misuse of Scripture can cause poverty. Every attempt to make godliness synonymous with poverty brings a believer against close to two thousand Scriptures and even God's method for operation. Two thirds of the thirty-nine parables of Jesus had to do with economics. So if you do not understand that the Scripture teaches being blessed, then you have a challenge.

Paul's reference to *contentment* means *to have satisfaction, to know fulfilment, to have joy and pleasure in life*. *Great gain* in that verse also means *huge profit, abundance, plenty*.

Let us look at two or three more Scriptures that are twisted by people with a beggar's mentality. The Scriptures say, "The love of money is the root of all evil", but it is misquoted as "Money is the root of all evil". That certainly is not true, because if it is, then the number one sin Christians commit is the pursuit of money, since they spend eight to nine hours working for themselves or an employer to earn money.

Some would infer other meanings into Romans 8:28 which says,

> *And we know that all things work together for good to them that love God, to them who are the called according to his purpose.*
> *Romans 8:28 (KJV)*

And make it sound as if that includes poverty, sickness and disease.

If poverty, sickness and disease would work together for good, God would have showered the whole world with more diseases, and Jesus would not have needed to die for our sickness and disease.

People with a beggar's mentality would also misuse the Scriptures and argue that rich people would not go to heaven, or that it would be hard for them to go to heaven.

The story of Lazarus is also used as an example, this certainly is a misused passage because there are three characters in that story, and the third person is Abraham. If the rich man did not make heaven because of his wealth, Abraham should not have, because we are told that he was 'very rich'.

And Abram was very rich in cattle, in silver, and in gold.
Genesis 13:2 (KJV)

Lazarus truly was poor, he made it to heaven, but so did Abraham. Lazarus only missed out on the blessings of God's wealth while he was on earth.

One more picture of a beggar's mentality was the man by the pool of Bethsaida, who when he was asked if he would be made whole, said, "I have no man". This means no contact, and no help.

People with a beggar's mentality justify their present predicament and condition by blaming their parents, their teachers, the educational system, and the government. Everyone is to blame but them. Some blame their colour or the lack of education.

Released balloons do not rise because of their colour, but the content of each one.

What did Bartimaeus do? And how did his change come?

SEEK CHANGE

There were lots of beggars on the way to Jericho on that great day when Jesus showed up. Of the three synoptic gospels that recorded this story, two give us the impression that only Bartimaeus wanted a change.

Nobody likes change, except babies in wet nappies.

It is the tendency of people when they have been in a rut for a long time to begin to justify it, and make 'sacred cows' out of things they should have abandoned or considered obsolete. The other beggars probably preferred where they where.

Money was coming in; sweatless money, but it was money based on hassling and hustling. Bartimaeus became tired of a dead end.

Until you lose sight of your present shore, you cannot discover a new harbour.

Others were contented with what they had; they kept playing the same game they have always played. But Bartimaeus smelt victory and he pressed in until he got it.

He cried until change came.

> *If a man die, shall he live again? all the days of my*
> *appointed time will I wait, till my change come.*
> *Job 14:14 (KJV)*

BECOME UNSTOPPABLE

Every time a man makes up his mind to make a change, there would be reactions from those who prefer the way it has always been.

The irony of life is that those who prefer us the way we have always been seem to be our friends and families, because it is most comfortable for them.

It is easier for them to manoeuvre around us in the state in which we used to be. They hate our unpredictability. They disdain our new move, our change, and our progress, it means they have to change. They prefer the disorder around us because it makes life comfortable for them.

Every time you raise your level of order, people's disorder around you is exposed; they will either change or there will be reactions.

People who do not like your new move will ridicule the light you have just seen. They will try to belittle your craving. They like the fact that you have acted the fool together, going nowhere together and settling for the 'rest' and not the 'best'. Unless you make up your mind to leave them behind, by the wailing walls of Jericho, they will hold you back where they are.

It is time to press in, press on and press hard.

I press toward the mark for the prize of the high calling of God in Christ Jesus.
Philippians 3:14 (KJV)

Can you blame Bartimaeus, he felt change, he sensed change, he decided he was going to be unstoppable. They tried to discourage him, shut him up, and silence him. But the more they tried, the uglier it became, and the louder his voice became. He lost his decorum and his cool; he became foolish for God because He knew that the difference between breaking barriers and being held in blindness, bondage and begging was to decide to become unstoppable.

COMMAND JESUS' ATTENTION

Heaven comes to attention when men on earth cry out of a heart that is truly seeking and searching. No cry goes unnoticed particularly a cry of a man for mercy.

Jesus stopped, heaven stopped, the angels stopped, the saints stopped. He gave His undivided attention to a man nobody had minded all his life. That is what makes Jesus different. That was what made Him different from the religious leaders of His time.

This man may not have looked the way he ought to have looked, he may not have smelled the way he ought to have, he may have walked badly and made mistakes wearing the wrong garment, but he did one right thing this fateful day. He cried for "mercy".

The number one prayer of any man who must have heaven's gates of splendour open to him is, "Lord be merciful unto me a sinner".

This man commanded Jesus' attention by his cry of mercy but also by his recognition of the season. Bartimaeus may not have known many things, but he knew that this was his season.

One of the challenges of our times is that we have raised a bunch of Christians who do not know the power of season; the appropriate time for things to happen.

I think Bartimaeus cried louder because he felt "This Man may not walk this way again. He may not do it like this again. This is my day to be brought out of blindness, bondage begging, this is my day to be brought in to all that God has for me". The riches of Christ that are unfathomable. The barrier must be broken; the line must be crossed.

And when Bartimaeus heard Him stop and call his name, he knew the barrier was over, he opened his mouth and called upon the Saviour. Once your mouth can call Him, then your ears will hear the change coming.

BREAKING FROM THE PAST

Remember we are talking about "Breaking Life's Barriers". Some have been with us from as far as we can remember, but you must tear up your identity card that ties you to where you used to come from. You cannot keep your identity card of your association of Jericho's blind, bound beggars.

Throw away darkness, put on light, and declare clearly that the barrier is broken and you have crossed Satan's line. You see, you are too good for the weight Satan wants to put upon you; depression, oppression, repression and suppression, you are too good for them.

Wherefore seeing we also are compassed about with so great a cloud of witnesses, let us lay aside every weight, and the sin which doth so easily beset us, and let us run with patience the race that is set before us,
Hebrews 12:1 (KJV)

You are too good for Satan's darkness.

As far as God is concerned when you embraced Christ, your blindness potentially ended, the darkness is over.

But put ye on the Lord Jesus Christ, and make not provision for the flesh, to fulfil the lusts thereof.
Romans 13:14 (KJV)

Arise, shine; for thy light is come, and the glory of the LORD is risen upon thee. For, behold, the darkness shall cover the earth, and gross darkness the people: but the LORD shall arise upon thee, and his glory shall be seen upon thee.
Isaiah 60:1-2 (KJV)

Bartimaeus' garments were a symbol of carnality, fleshly desires, evil concupiscence that satisfies the flesh and gets the approval of men, but stops the hand of God and slows you down on the race to the best of God. It is time to declare to it "I am too good for this mess".

Mortify therefore your members which are upon the earth; fornication, uncleanness, inordinate affection, evil concupiscence, and covetousness, which is idolatry: For which things' sake the wrath of God cometh on the children of disobedience:
Colossians 3:5-6 (KJV)

These things are a bondage and a barrier, it is time to break free and walk in the new light available to you. You cannot stay in the old joint any more, the Jericho strip where they used to know you. Rise today and declare "I've broken the barriers, now I'm a barrier breaker and a line crosser".

CHAPTER FOUR

RECEIVING THE BARRIER BREAKER'S SPIRIT

We have argued continuously in this book on the need for you to see barriers broken in your life and changes that affect every facet.

It is not enough to see yourself wanting to come out of bondages and yokes, it is important to allow the anointing which breaks the barriers to rest permanently upon your life.

For your individual victory and for the corporate victory you can bring for others.

The barrier breaker's spirit is necessary because the enemy only departs for a season. We are told in the case of Jesus, that when he was resisted by our Lord, he only departed for a season.

What will make your victory permanent and make you go from victory to victory, is when you have a barrier breaker's spirit resting upon your life.

We have an interesting reference in Nehemiah 11:4, 6 to the family of Perez. They were addressed as "valiant men". The name Perez is at the root of every word that has to do with *breaking or breaker*.

If we must win, we must have the anointing of the people called Perez.

CHARACTERISTICS OF A BARRIER BREAKER'S SPIRIT

THEY ARE VALIANT MEN

And such as do wickedly against the covenant shall he corrupt by flatteries: but the people that do know their God shall be strong, and do exploits.
Daniel 11:32 (KJV)

Through God we shall do valiantly: for he it is that shall tread down our enemies.
Psalms 60:12 (KJV)

THEY ARE FORCEFUL MEN

There are also 'forceful men'. In the last days, the kingdom of God would only be made to advance by 'forceful men'.

Only forceful violent men would take the kingdom of the enemy by force.

This violence of course relates to holy violence; tearing down Satan's kingdom.

THEY ARE PROSPEROUS MEN

People with a barrier breaker's spirit are also 'prosperous men'. They overpower by reason of the blessing of the Blesser, which rests upon their lives.

Nehemiah 11:6 shows us that Perez were only ten percent of all those who dwelt in the city in the days of Nehemiah. But if you have a barrier breaker's spirit, you would understand that ten percent of God is enough to execute His purpose.

It is also a mirror of those who have been sanctified and set apart by God to do specific things and carry out specific assignments. If you have the spirit of a barrier breaker things begin to change around you.

They execute the change of God; they do not accept every circumstance as being normal or beyond change. They expect the wind of change to blow, wherever they go.

THE PROBLEMS THEY CONFRONT

When the barrier breaker's anointing is upon your life, you are able to boldly confront and defeat whatever challenges you,
or brings a battle against you or what you love.

Those who have a barrier breaker's spirit know that the weapons of the enemy are not a match at all, with all of the greatness of the armoury of God available to the believer.

(For the weapons of our warfare are not carnal, but mighty through God to the pulling down of strong holds;)
Casting down imaginations, and every high thing that exalteth itself against the knowledge of God, and bringing into captivity every thought to the obedience of Christ;
2 Corinthians 10:4-5 (KJV)

It is within this context that we must bring the weapons of God against:

SORROW

Therefore the redeemed of the LORD shall return, and come with singing unto Zion; and everlasting joy shall be upon their head: they shall obtain gladness and joy; and sorrow and mourning shall flee away.
Isaiah 51:11 (KJV)

The barrier breaker's spirit must also come against the grip of fear.

FEAR

We have mentioned it several times in this book, but it cannot be overemphasised. The necessity is there for the believer to realise that no matter how anointed you are, a spirit of fear would look for a weak point and try to come in there.

If it is not the fear of being blessed, it is the fear of being poor.

Some will not give or release what God has provided, because they are afraid they might go broke like their parents were once broke.

Let us bring the barrier breaker's spirit against worry.

WORRY

And the peace of God, which passeth all understanding, shall keep your hearts and minds through Christ Jesus.
Philippians 4:7 (KJV)

Worry makes a big thing out of a small thing.

Unless you have a barrier breaker's spirit, you could end up a world champion worrier.

Worry feeds our imagination, and takes advantage of our sometimes tired mind, and in such moments makes us launch out, finding an enemy that does not exist.

The barrier breaker's spirit is also necessary to come against the yokes of financial bondage.

Two-thirds of the world is living under poverty. Being born again is not enough. The benefits of salvation must be obtained.

If you do not have the barrier breaker's spirit, the mountains could just stay there and the financial hassles holding the believer could continue.

A breaker's spirit will make you to refuse to accept that financial hardship is business as usual.

You need the breaker's spirit that comes against the oppositions that want to annihilate you. Jesus told Peter "the enemy had meant to destroy you, but I have prayed for you".

And the Lord said, Simon, Simon, behold, Satan hath
desired to have you, that he may sift you as wheat:
But I have prayed for thee, that thy faith fail not: and when
thou art converted, strengthen thy brethren.
Luke 22:31-32 (KJV)

The kings of the earth gathered and plotted against Jesus.

The kings of the earth set themselves, and the rulers take
counsel together, against the LORD, and against his
anointed, saying, Let us break their bands asunder, and
cast away their cords from us. He that sitteth in the
heavens shall laugh: the Lord shall have them in derision.
Psalms 2:2-4 (KJV)

Those in opposition to Paul set an ambush to destroy him. It is your guaranteed weapon against jealousy, attacks, slander and every other arsenic weapon the enemy may roll out against you.

THE POSSIBILITIES FOR THE BARRIER BREAKER'S SPIRIT

When you have the barrier breaker's spirit, you are blessed and highly favoured.

You are like the man described in the Psalm 1.

Blessed is the man that walketh not in the counsel of the ungodly, nor standeth in the way of sinners, nor sitteth in the seat of the scornful. But his delight is in the law of the LORD; and in his law doth he meditate day and night. And he shall be like a tree planted by the rivers of water, that bringeth forth his fruit in his season; his leaf also shall not wither; and whatsoever he doeth shall prosper.
Psalms 1:1-3 (KJV)

So he becometh like a tree planted by the watercourses....
And its leaf withereth not
Psalm 1:3 (DeW)

......He stands firm as a tree planted by running water.....
Psalm 1:3 (Knox)

.....Which shall produce its fruit at the proper season...
Psalm 1:3 (Sprl)

.....and its fruit shall not fall untimely.....
Psalm 1:3 (Sept)

....and whose leaves never fade....
Psalm 1:3 (NAB)

.....And whatever it bears comes to maturity
Psalm 1:3 (AAT)

....and whatsoever he begins he accomplishes
Psalm 1:3 (Lam)

.....success attends all he does
Psalm 1:3 (Jerus)

.....In all that he does, he prospers
Psalm 1:3 (RSV)

......and he will do well in all his undertakings
Psalm 1:3 (Bas)

Blessed and fortunate and happy and spiritually prosperous
(in that state in which the born-again child of God enjoys
His favor and salvation) are those who hunger and thirst
for righteousness (up-rightness and right standing with
God), for they shall be completely satisfied.
Matthew 5:6 (Amplified)

Just as we have seen earlier in previous pages, the river Jordan, the walls of Jericho, the mountains of Sinai and many other challenges were a barrier to the Children of Israel. But when these barriers saw the Ark of the Lord and what it contained; The Tablets, the Rod and the Manna, each battle had to back off, each barrier had to become a blessing.

THE TABLETS

The tablets containing the Ten Commandments, the Word in the Ark of the Covenant – stood for the integrity and faithfulness of God.

The barrier breaker must know that God's Word has integrity and can stand the test of time.

The grass withereth, the flower fadeth: but the word of our God shall stand for ever.
Isaiah 40:8 (KJV)

So shall my word be that goeth forth out of my mouth: it shall not return unto me void, but it shall accomplish that which I please, and it shall prosper in the thing whereto I sent it.
Isaiah 55:11 (KJV)

THE ROD

The Rod stands for God's supernatural performance; He is still in the business of doing signs and wonders.

God forbid: yea, let God be true, but every man a liar; as it is written, That thou mightest be justified in thy sayings, and mightest overcome when thou art judged.
Romans 3:4 (KJV)

THE MANNA

The manna stands for God's perpetual provision. We have enough witnesses to know that if God promised it, He will make it good.

But my God shall supply all your need according to his riches in glory by Christ Jesus.
Philippians 4:19 (KJV)

It is in the light of this that Jordan had to part and Jericho had to fall, because the Ark of God was symbolic of God's anointing coming against barriers.

For the believer today, as you seek for God's anointing to rest upon your life – it certainly will bring down the yokes and the bondages.

And it shall come to pass in that day, that *his burden shall be taken away from off thy shoulder, and his yoke from off thy neck, and the yoke shall be destroyed because of the anointing.*
Isaiah 10:27 (KJV)

Our possibilities as barrier breakers are not based on good thoughts but the sure Word of God who promises to go before us, so that it is not what we confront, it is who goes with us.

I will go before thee, and make the crooked places straight: I will break in pieces the gates of brass, and cut in sunder the bars of iron:
Isaiah 45:2 (KJV)

This means in effect that God goes ahead of us in all battles and brings the victory He has promised us into manifestation.

No weapon that is formed against thee shall prosper; and every tongue that shall rise against thee in judgment thou shalt condemn. This is the heritage of the servants of the LORD, and their righteousness is of me, saith the LORD.
Isaiah 54:17 (KJV)

And they shall fight against thee; but they shall not prevail against thee; for I am with thee, saith the LORD, to deliver thee.
Jeremiah 1:19 (KJV)

And I will make thee unto this people a fenced brasen wall: and they shall fight against thee, but they shall not prevail against thee: for I am with thee to save thee and to deliver thee, saith the LORD.
Jeremiah 15:20 (KJV)

And he answered, Fear not: for they that be with us are more than they that be with them.
2 Kings 6:16 (KJV)

THE PRACTICE OF THE BARRIER BREAKER'S SPIRIT

BREAK THE BARRIERS

I will go before thee, and make the crooked places straight: I will break in pieces the gates of brass, and cut in sunder the bars of iron: And I will give thee the treasures of darkness, and hidden riches of secret places, that thou mayest know that I, the LORD, which call thee by thy name, am the God of Israel.
Isaiah 45:2-3 (KJV)

Do not behold the barriers, do not write about the barriers, do not write songs about the barriers, do not moan about the barriers, do not celebrate the barriers, do not package the barriers, do not overemphasise the barriers, just break them!

Not in your power, but as you pray to the Father, in the power of the Spirit, in the Name of Jesus, the barriers must be broken.

BREAK FORTH

Breaking forth is probably better understood if we go back to our earlier word *Perez*. In Genesis 2:14

And the name of the third river is Hiddekel: that is it which goeth toward the east of Assyria. And the fourth river is Euphrates.
Genesis 2:14 (KJV)

The fourth river Euphrates actually is derived from *Perez* or *Perizzim*. So it is *Eu-perizzim*. The river was said to 'break forth'.

God wants you to break forth when the anointing of the Holy Spirit rests upon you.

Since these are the days when the trickles of His anointing must stop and you should break forth like a river, what are you waiting for?

BREAK OUT

*And Jabez was more honourable than his brethren: and his
mother called his name Jabez, saying, Because I bare him
with sorrow. And Jabez called on the God of Israel,
saying, Oh that thou wouldest bless me indeed, and
enlarge my coast, and that thine hand might be with me,
and that thou wouldest keep me from evil, that it may not
grieve me! And God granted him that which he requested.*
1 Chronicles 4:9-10 (KJV)

The people we see affect us, they determine who we become, they determine what we hear and they shape our vision.

Jabez's mother in this story allowed her immediate
limitations, challenges and barriers to shape her
vision of the future, so she called her son
'sorrow'.

It was left to him to allow his mother's opinion
and possibly that of relatives to hold him where he
was, but Jabez thought differently, he cried to the
Lord.

*And Jabez called on the God of Israel, saying, Oh that
thou wouldest bless me indeed, and enlarge my coast, and
that thine hand might be with me, and that thou wouldest*

keep me *from evil, that it may not grieve me! And God
granted him that which he requested.*
1 Chronicles 4:10 (KJV)

God granted his request.

So my friend, break out, do not let any one stop
you, limit you or put a hold on where you should
reach.

*The breaker is come up before them: they have broken up,
and have passed through the gate, and are gone out by it:
and their king shall pass before them, and the LORD on
the head of them.*
Micah 2:13 (KJV)

Lastly God wants you to Break Through.

BREAK THROUGH

*And David came to Baalperazim, and David smote them
there, and said, The LORD hath broken forth upon mine
enemies before me, as the breach of waters. Therefore he
called the name of that place Baalperazim.*
2 Samuel 5:20 (KJV)

With the barrier breaker's spirit, some things may
be hard to break into, others may not want you to
break forth or break out from, but as you allow

the mantle and grace of the Lord upon your life, you will tear down prison doors and everything that wants to stop you.

The Spirit of the Lord GOD is upon me; because the LORD hath anointed me to preach good tidings unto the meek; he hath sent me to bind up the brokenhearted, to proclaim liberty to the captives, and the opening of the prison to them that are bound; To proclaim the acceptable year of the LORD, and the day of vengeance of our God; to comfort all that mourn; To appoint unto them that mourn in Zion, to give unto them beauty for ashes, the oil of joy for mourning, the garment of praise for the spirit of heaviness; that they might be called trees of righteousness, the planting of the LORD, that he might be glorified.
Isaiah 61:1-3 (KJV)

TESTIMONIES

6th August 2000 - Breaking Barriers Sunday evening service. - I crossed the line.

Pastor Matthew talked about buying a house. He said a prophetic statement, I believed and it happened to me just as he had said it. The house price was reduced! They came back looking for me to buy the house! Praise God.

My first house I have bought and more so after a prophetic announcement. I'm blessed and highly favoured. I believed God for just a shelter over my head, a place to which to call my own and he provided a palace:

> 5 Bed roomed double story house;
> 4 Bathrooms and 6 Toilets;
> Dining Room;
> Kitchen, Pantry, Scullery,
> Laundry;
> 3 Bed roomed Cottage outside;
> Garages for 6 cars;
> Swimming Pool;
> Gazebo & 2 Satellite dishes;
> Durawalled and remote controlled gate.

This is just part of what God is doing in my life.
I am receiving favour from every angle of my life.
P M

The God of miracles performed His miracle in my life on Friday 30th March, 01.

I went to the Sainsbury Sava centre in Beckton, London to wash my car; with me in the car were my three children. We all put on our seat belts and my 4-year-old prayed because it was her turn to pray. She asked for God's protection. My car is fully automatic, if any of the doors were not properly shut it will indicate, you cannot open the boot if the engine is on, unless the person on the driver seat opens it. I was driving on the highway between 35 to 40 miles per hour, all traffic lights were on green with cars in front and behind me.

Suddenly, drivers were blaring their horns, and one in particular drove towards me and I looked at him to see what he was up to, he then signalled to me to look back, then I saw my boot widely open, I quickly parked the car to see what has happened. To my shock my 5 & 4-year-old-children had been sucked out of the car over 100 metres away from where I parked. Suddenly they came running from 100 metres towards me in the middle of the road on a very busy day. All the cars behind, on the left and right were at a stand still.

There was not a single scratch found on them; no sign of any dirt or particles on the road was found on their clothing. The fact that they fell from a moving car at the speed of 35-40 miles per hour, was enough to kill them instantly, the cars behind could have ran them over. But God put His angels charge over my children.

The enemy opened the boot to kill my children, but the LORD turned it to my testimony. He sent His angels to bear them up in their hands, just as He said in Psalm 91:11,12. I promised my God on the roadside that, the whole world will hear about this miracle. **O S**

God Does Take Care of our Finances

My wife and I had a flat repossessed approximately 10 years ago. Approximately 3 years ago after becoming Christians, we received a letter from our lenders saying that we owed them £36,000.00.

They stated that they required £250.00 pounds per month, but they agreed to a payment of £70.00 per month. I never missed a payment but I realised that at £70.00 per month it would take almost 43 years to clear the debt.

Approximately three months ago I was in my car and I was listening to the radio. I was not supposed to be in the car, but I was doing someone a favour. Pastor Matthew was talking about finance and he stated that if you have a debt, write or call the creditors making them an offer to settle the debt. I thought straight away I must try that.

I prayed about what Pastor Matthew said and decided to make an offer to settle the debt. I made an offer of £1,500.00. A week later I received a letter stating that they were considering my offer. I received a letter a week later stating they were unable to accept £1,500.00 but would accept £3,000.00.

I thank God because well over £30,000.00 was cancelled. I sent the building society a cheque for £3,000.00 and I received a reply last week to say the debt has been settled.

P & D C

Dear Pastor Ashimolowo,

I thank my God for KICC, where my family grows continually in faithfulness to God. I thank God for uncountable daily miracles, and I wish to share some of the testimonies.

I thank God because as I have put my trust in Him, He has never let me down. Sometimes, answers to my prayers have been delayed, but God always comes through with much more than I asked for.

As Pastor Matthew has encouraged repeatedly, I have put God to test with my tithe and offerings, and I have continuously witnessed God's divine intervention in my life and family. My family has never been broke, despite the fact that everyone around us has had to wait for their pay-day.

My husband has been blessed with miraculous contract jobs. And we completely paid off our mortgage after 3 & ½ years.

I had being praying for 2 years to change my career to one in IT, expecting to start with an increase of £5,000 maximum, but I got a good one near home, and with an increase of £12,500 + so many extra benefits. God is true, He is good, and this is only the beginning!

C O